New Techniques for Machine Quilting and Assembly—

Block by Block

That Patchwork Place®

Beth Donaldson

Credits

Editor-in-Chief .... Barbara Weiland
Technical Editors .... Kerry I. Hoffman
Melissa Lowe
Managing Editor .... Greg Sharp
Copy Editor ....Liz McGehee
Proofreader .... Leslie Phillips
Illustrator .... Brian Metz
Illustration Assistant................... Lisa McKenney
Photographer ....Brent Kane
Photographer's Assistant............ Richard Lipshay
Design Director .... Judy Petry
Text and Cover Designer .... Cheryl Stevenson
Design Assistant .... Claudia L'Heureux

Library of Congress Cataloging-in-Publication Data
Donaldson, Beth,
    Block by block : new techniques for machine quilting and
assembly / Beth Donaldson.4
        p.   cm.
    Includes bibliographical references and indexes.
    ISBN 1-56477-079-6
    1. Machine quilting—Patterns. 2. Patchwork—Patterns.
I. Title.
TT835.D662   1995
746.46—dc20
                                    95-12434
                                    CIP

Acknowledgments

A big thank you to: Mary Ellen Sample, who is my
sister, therapist, and the best seamstress I know; Joan
Kolodziej, my mom, who has always provided me
with humor, fabric, patterns, and a place to sew;
Chester Kolodziej, my dad, whose love of learning
and organization I inherited; the staff and students
of Country Stitches in East Lansing, Michigan,
where I developed these patterns and methods; the
Capitol City Quilt Guild quilters, who have inspired
me each month for the last ten years; Sherlee Mauch,
my mentor and a tireless supporter of quilting; Pep-
per Cory, my first quilt teacher; Debbi Brunner,
Michelle Mitchell, and Mary Ellen Sample, for their
beautiful quilts; the Northern House quilters: Hanne
Allen, Norine Antuck, Colleen Beach, Marti
Caterino, Pat Clark, Madonna Ferguson, Pat Linnell,
Irene Pavlik, Dee Pearson, Linda Plyler, Lennie
Rathbun, Carol Schon, Jackie Shulsky, Suzy Speck,
and Marie Van Tilburg; Ruth Dukelow, for help with
copyright information; the magicians at That
Patchwork Place, who turned my rough patterns into
the beautiful book you see here; and Jennifer Otto
and Kristen Stark, for their constant friendship
and support.

Dedication

To my husband, Tom, who never doubted my abil-
ity to write this book and to my children, Katy and
Colleen, who remind me daily that there is more to
life than quilting.

Contents

Introduction

A quiltmaker since high school, I began teaching quiltmaking classes in 1985 and started designing my own patterns in 1990. Anyone who has taught knows that teaching is the best way to learn! Helping others solve their problems challenges you to find different approaches and work from different points of view.

When I couldn't find patterns that combined all of the techniques I wanted to teach in one class, I began designing my own. I combined traditional quilt blocks with the latest rotary cutting, machine quilting, and "quilt-as-you-go" techniques.

Traditionally, the emphasis of "quilt-as-you-go" has been on portability; it's a way to carry your quilt project with you in small pieces and hand quilt while waiting in doctors' offices, traveling on airplanes, or anyplace where space is limited.

Since I wanted to machine quilt, my problem was not portability; it was weight. I could machine quilt small pieces to my satisfaction, but dealing with the weight and bulk of larger projects made me miserable. Also, my machine quilting didn't look as good on larger projects. I needed to machine quilt small pieces, then sew them together to make the quilt.

I worked on these challenges until I developed my own Block by Block machine-quilting method. It's fast and easy, and the results are beautiful! I've been teaching my method since 1990, and I've received encouragement and praise from the quiltmakers who have used it.

Whether you are just beginning or have been making quilts for many years, I hope that you enjoy my method and this book.

Getting Started

This block-by-block method is the result of my efforts to find a quick and easy way to piece, assemble, and quilt a group of blocks entirely by machine. It eliminates the hand finishing required with the traditional "quilt-as-you-go" method as well as the frustration and hassle often associated with machine quilting a completed quilt top.

The success of the machine-assembly-and-quilting method relies on using a quilt setting with corners and sashings around each block. Each of the blocks included in this book measures 12½" x 12½" (12" finished). Each corner measures 3½" x 3½" (3" x 3" finished), and each sashing measures 3½" x 12½" (3" x 12" finished). Once you have made a quilt using this technique, you will find that the basic assembly method is easy to adapt for other sizes of blocks, corners, and sashings.

In "Settings," beginning on page 70, you will find a variety of ways to make corners and sashings. A cutting chart and an assembly diagram are included for each variation. You can use plain corners or more complex variations, such as Four-Patch, Nine-Patch, Pinwheel, or Mini-star corners. You can combine any of these corners with plain, double, or triple sashings. Choose the corner and sashing combination that best sets off your blocks. Several possible combinations are shown below.

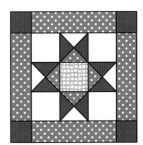

Plain Corners
and Sashing

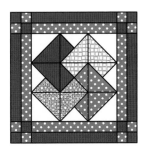

Four-Patch Corners
and Double Sashing

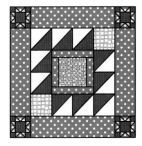

Mini-star Corners
and Plain Sashing

Nine-Patch Corners
and Triple Sashing

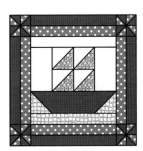

Pinwheel Corners
and Double Sashing

Using my method, you piece the blocks and then add sashings and corners in a prescribed order. Once you have pieced the blocks, sashings, and corner units, you layer each one with batting and backing, then quilt and assemble by machine. The actual assembly and quilting are intertwined; you sew blocks together in rows and then sew the rows together to complete the quilt. The process may appear tricky when you read through the directions the first time, but it's far easier and faster than it looks or sounds! Study the illustrations for the four-block quilt shown below to get a general idea of how the method works. Each step is explained in detail in the sections that follow. For more information on assembling the quilt, refer to page 82.

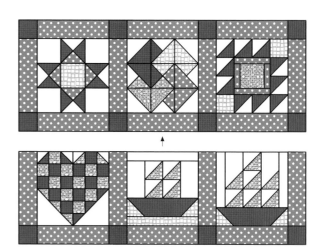

Sew the blocks together, then sew the rows together.

Make the blocks and add sashing and corner squares.

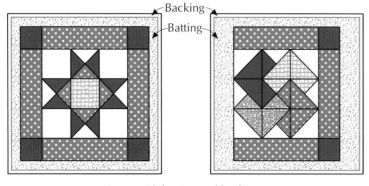

Backing

Batting

Layer with batting and backing.

Planning Your Quilt

Now that you have a general understanding of how to make a quilt block by block, it's time to plan your quilt project. First, decide on the quilt size you wish to make, using your favorite 12" (finished size) block designs. Choose from the twenty-five blocks featured on pages 24–69. Each of these blocks measures 12½" x 12½" and finishes to 12" square. To see these blocks used in finished quilts, refer to the "Gallery of Quilts" on pages 13–20.

You can substitute other favorite 12" finished block designs if you prefer, but I recommend you start with some of those featured in this book. I have included piecing and pressing directions that ensure easy machine quilting.

Choose a variety of blocks to make a sampler quilt like "Stars in My Corner" (page 14), or repeat one block many times to develop a theme as in "Northern Houses" (page 16). Another possibility is to repeat two different blocks with designs that connect at the corners to create the illusion of blocks set on point. "Ships That Pass in the Night" (page 17) is a good example of this design technique. As you plan your quilt, you will soon realize that the possibilities are endless.

This book includes instructions for eight different quilt sizes: table runner, wall, crib, lap, twin, full, queen, and king. Refer to the "Quilt Size Chart" below for the approximate dimensions for each size. Remember, the finished dimensions of your quilt may vary slightly based on your stitching accuracy, your batting choice, and the amount of quilting.

You can make your quilt with or without borders. If necessary, you can adjust the width of the borders to customize the quilt for your bed. See "Borders" on pages 86–88.

Be realistic as you plan your first block-by-block quilt. Even when you use the latest sewing tools and machines in combination with easy methods like mine, making a large quilt is a considerable undertaking. If you hurry, you won't achieve the results you want. Remember that it's the tools and methods we use that make quiltmaking faster and easier, not the rate at which we use them. (See "Tools and Supplies" on pages 11–12 for more information on the tools you will need.)

Tip

If you are a beginning quiltmaker, start with some of the simpler blocks and make a four-block table runner or wall hanging. As your confidence grows, try more difficult blocks and larger quilts.

Quilt Size Chart

	Runner	Wall	Crib	Lap	Twin	Full	Queen	King
Dimensions (without border)	18½" x 63½"	33½" x 33½"	33½" x 48½"	48½" x 63½"	48½" x 78½"	63½" x 78½"	63½" x 78½"	78½" x 78½"
Dimensions (with borders)	27½" x 72½"	45½" x 45½"	45½" x 60½"	64½" x 79½"	64½" x 94½"	79½" x 94½"	85½" x 100½"	100½" x 100½"

Determining Yardage

As you plan your quilt, refer to the "Quilt Plan" on page 8. I recommend that you decide on the size of your quilt (the number of blocks you need), then select the fabrics for your blocks. After you've made the blocks, refer to "Settings" on pages 70–78, to choose the corner and sashing designs and fabrics that work best with your blocks.

Refer to the "Block by Block Quilt Planner" on page 10. Each time you plan a new quilt, make a photocopy of this quilt planner and use it to stay organized.

After you have decided on the quilt size you wish to make and the number of blocks required, determine how much fabric you need by referring to the "Block Yardage Chart" on page 8. You may also want to read "Selecting Your Fabrics," beginning on page 9, before you head for the fabric store. Record the necessary amounts of each fabric in the appropriate boxes on the quilt planner.

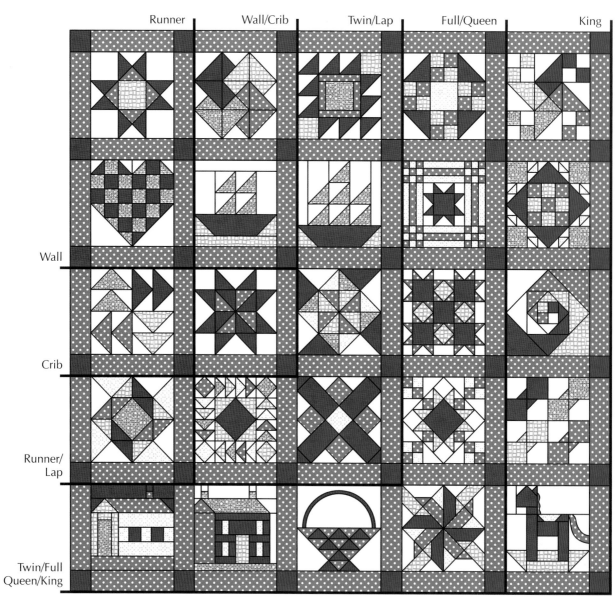

Wall

Crib

Runner/
Lap

Twin/Full
Queen/King

Quilt Plan

Block Yardage Chart

Materials: 44"-wide fabric • Fabric Requirements in Yards

	Runner/Wall	Crib	Lap	Twin	Full/Queen	King
Number of Blocks	4	6	12	15	20	25
Fabric						
Main	½	¾	1½	2	2½	3
Background	½	¾	1½	2	2½	3
Accents (at least four different fabrics)	¼*	¼*	⅜	½	⅝	¾

*You can also use fat quarters.

When you have finished your blocks and decided on the setting you will use, calculate the yardage requirements for the corners and sashings and add this information to the planner. Finally, select the fabrics for the borders and binding. See "Borders" on pages 86–88 and "Binding" on pages 89–90.

Take the planner to the quilt shop each time you shop for fabrics for your quilt. As the clerk cuts your fabrics, ask for a little swatch of each and tape the swatches in the appropriate boxes on the chart.

When selecting fabrics, I like to buy what is listed in the "Block Yardage Chart" (page 8) and then supplement the accent fabrics with pieces from my stash. Feel free to add different accent fabrics as you go. You may wander into the local quilt shop one day and find a new fabric that is the perfect addition to your quilt!

Selecting Your Fabrics

You can use any type of fabric you like, but I recommend using 100% cotton. Take your time when selecting fabric. Your fabric defines the style, color, and impact of your quilt.

After helping my students select fabric for hundreds of quilts, I've come up with a simple formula. Select a main fabric, a background fabric, and at least four different accent fabrics.

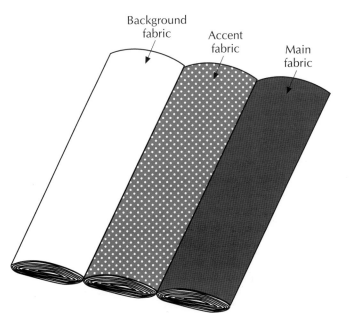

The Main Fabric

Choose your main fabric first. It should evoke the style you want for your quilt; it is the focus of your design. The print on this fabric usually looks bright or busy, or is larger than the other prints in your quilt. Use the main fabric in the block areas that you want to stand out, such as the points of a star as shown in the Devil's Claw block below. You may also want to use the main fabric for the border, backing, and binding.

Consider using a main fabric with a theme. For example, a bright fabric patterned with teddy bears would make a great children's quilt.

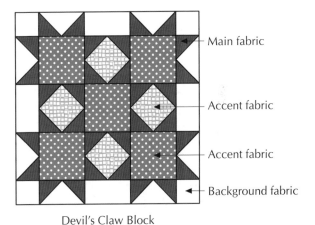

Devil's Claw Block

The Background Fabric

The background fabric contrasts with the main fabric. A background print should be subtle and look as if it recedes when you stand away from it. Choose a tiny, tone-on-tone print in one of the shades found in your main fabric. A dark tone-on-tone print works wonderfully with a bright, multicolor main print. You can also use more than one background fabric or color.

The Accent Fabrics

The accent fabrics enhance the colors in your main fabric and add variety and texture to your quilt. Choose medium- and small-scale, tone-on-tone, or geometric prints in the colors of your main fabric. Use the accent fabrics in the corners and sashings. They add interest to the quilt without overpowering the blocks and borders.

BLOCK BY BLOCK QUILT PLANNER

QUILT SIZE (See pages 7–8.)	MAIN (See page 9.)	ACCENTS–choose at least four (See pages 9 and 11.)	BACK-GROUND (See page 9.)	CORNERS (See pages 70–74 and 77–78.)	SASHING (See pages 75–78.)	BACKING (See page 79.)	FIRST BORDER (See page 86.)	SECOND BORDER (See pages 86–88.)	BINDING (See pages 89–90.)
FABRIC AMOUNTS IN YARDS									
SWATCHES									

Small-scale prints with high-contrast designs look spotty from a distance. They are difficult to work with as a background fabric but often add just the right touch as an accent fabric.

Don't worry about whether every accent fabric looks good with each of the others. They only need to look good with the main fabric. There are often several places in a block where the accent fabrics are not next to each other. Also, you might not use all the accent fabrics in every block in your quilt.

Fabric Preparation

Be sure to prewash, dry, and press your fabrics before using them. To prewash fabric, sort it into piles of like colors. Wash each group of fabrics in warm water with a mild soap. Shake the wrinkles free in each piece of wet fabric; then dry and press before cutting.

Tip

The secret to color is not whether the color is right or wrong, but how it reacts with the other colors in the quilt. Spread out the bolts next to each other, then stand back and look at them from a distance. This perspective helps you see the effect of the color combination.

Tools and Supplies

I have been making quilts and collecting tools for more than ten years. I don't expect you to run out and buy every tool that I use, so I divided my list into two categories: the bare necessities and the fun extras.

Bare Necessities

These are the tools and supplies that are essential for making these quilts. They include a sewing machine in good working order, a rotary cutter and mat, a 6½" x 24" rotary-cutting ruler, an 8" Bias Square® ruler, a 3" x 18" C-Thru® ruler for drawing lines, a pair of good sharp scissors, thread that blends with your fabrics, straight pins, a seam ripper, a sharp #2 lead pencil (for marking light fabrics), a sharp light-colored pencil (for marking dark fabrics), chalk pencils, and batting.

If you want to make the Hanging Basket block (page 61), you will need a compass to make the curved handle.

Sewing Machine

All sewing machines are different and some are better for machine quilting than others. I use a Bernina® sewing machine with a walking foot, an attachment that helps feed the layers of fabric through the machine evenly. This foot is especially helpful if you are using polyester batting.

Thread

Use good-quality thread. For piecing blocks, I use a thread that blends with my block fabrics. For machine quilting, I use 100% cotton sewing thread, rather than invisible nylon thread, and change the color of the top thread to match my quilt block. I use a color that matches my backing fabric in the bobbin.

Basting Pins

For pin basting, I recommend using flat, flower-head straight pins. The flat heads are easier to maneuver around when you are machine quilting.

Batting

I encourage you to experiment with different battings. Read the batting manufacturer's recom-mendations for information on the amount of quilting needed.

Polyester battings do not need a lot of quilting, but they do need to be heavily basted because the layers tend to slip as they pass through the sewing machine. Polyester battings are also more difficult to measure and cut.

Battings with a high cotton content (80% or 100%) hold the layers together and are a joy to machine quilt, but they usually need more quilt-ing than a polyester batting.

You can buy batting in packaged sizes or by the yard. (Refer to the Batting Yardage Chart below.) I like to buy batting by the yard from 90"-wide rolls. Because you cut the batting to fit each block, buying it by the yard is more cost-effective.

Batting Yardage Chart

	Runner/Wall	Crib	Lap	Twin	Full	Queen/King
Package	72" x 90"	72" x 90"	72" x 90"	90" x 108"	120" x 120"	72" x 90" and 90" x 108"
90"-wide Roll (yds.)	1¼	1½	3¼	3	4	4½

Fun Extras

Add these fun extras to the tools mentioned above. A ¼"-wide presser foot makes piecing accurate seam allowances easier. A 4½" x 14" ruler is easier to handle than the 6½" x 24" size when you're cutting small pieces. Also available are 4" and 6" Bias Square rulers. I like to use 1" x 12" or 1" x 6" rulers when I cut diagonal lines. The ScrapMaster ruler is handy when I just want to cut one triangle. Thread nippers are great for cutting between chain-pieced units and are handy for clipping threads. I keep a pair next to my machine at all times.

Gallery of Quilts

Snail's Trail
Block
(page 48)

Samurai Dance by Debbi Brunner, 1994, Williamston, Michigan, 48½" x 63½". The Japanese-inspired sashing fabric is the boldest fabric in this quilt and brings together the colors of the different plaids. Debbi chose the Snail's Trail block because it is also an ancient motif found in Japanese art. Hand quilted.

Stars in My Corner by Beth Donaldson, 1994, Lansing, Michigan, 79½" x 91½". Mini-star corners add sparkle to this full-size sampler.

Prairie Queen Block (page 29)	Goose on the Loose Block (page 51)	Diamond Star Block (page 43)	Rocky Mountain Puzzle Block (page 27)
Hanging Basket Block (page 61)	Saltbox House Block (page 59)	Devil's Claw Block (page 47)	Checkered Heart Block (page 32)
Album Block (page 52)	Mother's Fancy Star Block (page 38)	Bow Ties Block (page 56)	Variable Star Block (page 24)
Peace and Plenty Block (page 44)	Card Trick Block (page 25)	Dutchman's Puzzle Block (page 42)	Windblown Square Block (page 50)
Tall Ship Block (page 36)	Our Galaxy Block (page 30)	Schoolhouse Block (page 57)	Summer's Dream Block (page 39)

Block Key for Stars in My Corner

Painted Ponies by Beth Donaldson, 1994, Lansing, Michigan, 45½" x 60½". Made with brightly colored Rocking Horse blocks, pinwheel corners, and double sashings, this is a fun quilt any child would love.

Rocking Horse Block (page 66)

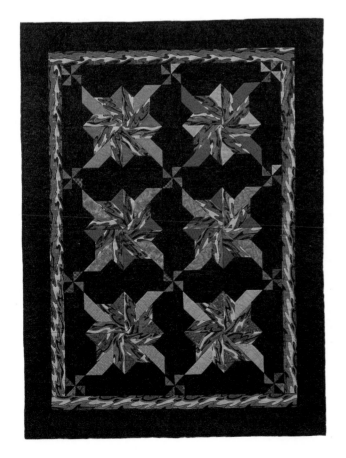

Whirling Star Block (page 64)

Whirling Stars by Beth Donaldson, 1994, Lansing, Michigan, 45½" x 60½". I used a bold fabric in each block and the first border. The stars appear to float because the sashing fabric is the same as the background fabric.

Saltbox
House
Block
(page 59)

Northern Houses by Beth Donaldson and friends, 1994, Lansing, Michigan, 64½"x 94½". I belong to a group of quilters who meet every Wednesday, and many of them have done beautiful quilts using a folk-art palette. When I wanted a quilt in these colors, I knew just who to ask! From top to bottom rows, left to right, the quilters are: Pat Clark, Hanne Allen, Jackie Shulsky, Dee Pearson, Suzy Speck, Lennie Rathbun, Colleen Beach, Pat Linnell, Marie Van Tilburg, Norine Antuck, Madonna Ferguson, Linda Plyler, Irene Pavlik, Carol Schon, and Marti Caterino.

Ships That Pass in the Night by Beth Donaldson, 1994, Lansing, Michigan, 85½" x 100½". I wanted to give the illusion that I had set the blocks on point, so I added four-patch corners to match the corners in the Sailor's Star blocks and used fabric that blended with the backgrounds for the sashings. This created the diagonal chain running through the quilt.

Sailboat Block (page 35)	Sailor's Star Block (page 54)

Prairie Queen Block (page 29)	Variable Star Block (page 24)
Dutchman's Puzzle Block (page 42)	Album Block (page 52)
Rocky Mountain Puzzle Block (page 27)	Card Trick Block (page 25)

Sea and Sand by Beth Donaldson, 1995, Lansing, Michigan, 45½" x 60½". Double sashing and Four-Patch corners allow you to alternate background fabrics in this soft and lovely quilt.

Strawberry Sundae by Mary Ellen Sample, 1995, Key Largo, Florida, 18½" x 63½". Shades of red and creamy white add festive fun to any table.

Christmas Eve by Beth Donaldson, 1995, Lansing, Michigan, 45½" x 60½". Classic red and green fabric and Mini-star corners create a beautiful holiday heirloom.

Sailor's
Star
Block
(page 54)

Our Galaxy
Block
(page 30)

Mother's
Fancy Star
Block
(page 38)

Rocky Moun-
tain Puzzle
Block
(page 27)

Peace and
Plenty
Block
(page 44)

Beginner's Sampler by Michelle Mitchell, 1994, Lapeer, Michigan, 45½" x 45½". The blocks for this quilt offer a wide range of techniques in a small project. The empty basket is the perfect place to personalize your quilt with hand quilting, appliqué, or a written message.

Diamond Star Block (page 43)	Schoolhouse Block (page 57)
Hanging Basket Block (page 61)	Our Galaxy Block (page 30)

The Blocks

The twenty-five quilt blocks in this section are all squares that measure 12½" x 12½" after the pieces are stitched together.

There are blocks for every skill level. The easiest blocks are indicated by a ✦.

Each block includes an illustration that indicates placement of the pieces cut from the main, background (light), or accent fabrics. Refer to pages 9–11 for a discussion on fabric selection. It's difficult to go wrong if you follow my suggestions.

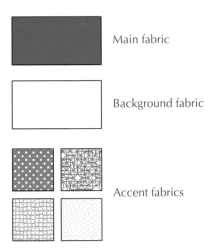

Main fabric

Background fabric

Accent fabrics

Each block pattern also includes an illustration with a letter (A, B, C, etc.) inside each piece. The letters correspond with the cutting directions and their placement in the block.

Yardage requirements vary for each block. Refer to "Determining Yardage" on page 7.

At the end of the directions for each block, you will find a "Quilting Suggestion." The machine quilting for each block was planned so that you start and stop and start again as few times as possible. You can actually machine quilt some of the blocks in a continuous line without stopping and starting again. The numbers and arrows indicate the order and direction in which to stitch.

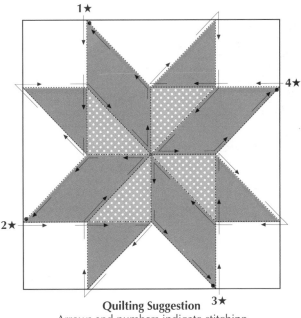

Quilting Suggestion
Arrows and numbers indicate stitching direction and order. See page 80.

After you have completed each block, you will add the sashing and corner squares, layer with batting and backing, quilt the block following the "Quilting Suggestion" given with the block, and then assemble the quilt, following the directions beginning on page 82.

Hints for Accurate Piecing

1. All seam allowances are ¼" wide. To maintain accurate and consistent ¼"-wide seams, use a ¼" quiltmaking presser foot on your sewing machine or mark an accurate ¼"-wide sewing guide on your machine.

Use graph paper with a ¼" grid to determine the measurement and mark the guide. Place a piece of masking tape or moleskin on the plate of the machine, being careful not to cover the feed dogs.

I prefer to set the stitch length at 15 stitches per inch; however, many quiltmakers use 10 to 12 stitches per inch. Stitch two strips of fabric together, then measure the seam allowance to check the width. Make adjustments to achieve accurate seam allowances.

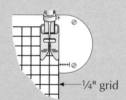

←¼" grid

Use ¼" graph paper to locate a new seam guide.

Put masking tape in front of needle along edge of graph paper to guide fabric.

2. Chain piecing is a great way to save time and thread and makes your piecing neater. Place the pieces that are to be joined right sides together. Feed under the presser foot, one after the other, making a chain of pieces. When you are done, clip the units apart and press. Start and end each chain with a scrap of fabric. The scrap will absorb any oil that may be on the needle and helps avoid puckered seams.

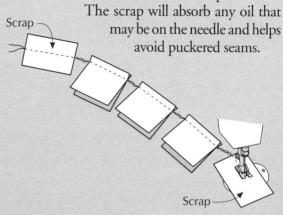

Scrap

Scrap

3. It is important to carefully align pieces before you sew them together. Make sure raw edges match and that right sides are together. If two units are supposed to be the same size and they do not match properly, you know that you made a mistake and need to make adjustments. Correct the mistake by removing the stitches in a seam and adjusting the seam width in the next step, or just relax your standards!

There are hints sprinkled throughout the blocks section that tell you how to align the shapes.

4. When marking stitching lines on fabric, use a *sharp* pencil and a C-Thru ruler. Do not use rotary-cutting rulers, because the thick acrylic casts shadows, which cause your markings to be inaccurate.

5. Check measurements and correct mistakes as you go. The block directions give the size of a unit (including the seam allowances) and the number of units you need. This prevents any unwelcome surprises when you are ready to assemble the block.

6. When a unit is completed, there are often little tips of fabric that extend beyond the edges of the unit. Trim the excess fabric tips away for neater and flatter patchwork.

Cutting Squares

Use the Bias Square® ruler to cut squares. Place the Bias Square on the corner of your pressed fabric. Make the first two cuts slightly longer than required by the block instructions.

Rotate the fabric 180°, so the just-cut sides align with the ruler markings for the required block size. Cut the remaining two sides. Your square is now finished. Check for accuracy. When there are many squares required, you may cut strips, then crosscut them into the required number of squares. The strip length given in the block instructions is slightly longer than needed to cut the required number of squares.

Cutting Triangles

Most of the triangles in this book are cut from squares. To cut any triangle, begin by cutting a square as described above.

To cut two triangles from a square, place the 45° diagonal line of the Bias Square on the left edge of the fabric square. Make sure the cutting edge of the Bias Square aligns exactly, from corner to corner, on your fabric square. Cut on the diagonal of the square to make two triangles.

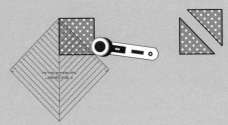

Some block instructions require that squares be cut twice diagonally, to yield four triangles. For these triangles, make the first cut as described above. Then, carefully cut again on the opposite diagonal.

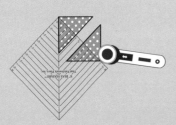

Pressing Tips

Pressing is one of the most important steps in quiltmaking. In patchwork, I have more accurate results when seams are pressed to one side. The directions for each block tell you which way to press the seams to ensure the flattest seams.

Press carefully to avoid distorting the shapes. If you have sewn a number of pieces together to form a square, then "think square" while you are pressing. It may even help you to lay a square piece of graph paper on your ironing board to help you visualize the shapes until you get used to thinking of pressing in this way.

It is especially important to press bias edges gently. Once they are stretched, they do not return to their original shape. Finger-press first before you press with a hot iron. Finger pressing is more accurate than pressing with an iron. Your sense of touch helps you to press seams completely that you might otherwise miss when you rely on your eyesight alone. I lay my patches on the ironing board, finger-press them, then press with a steam iron.

Variable Star

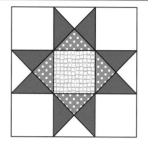
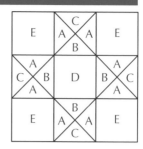

Cutting

- From the fabric for A, cut 2 squares, each 5¼" x 5¼".
  Cut each square twice diagonally to yield 8 triangles.
- From the fabric for B, cut 1 square, 5¼" x 5¼".
  Cut the square twice diagonally to yield 4 triangles.
- From the fabric for C, cut 1 square, 5¼" x 5¼".
  Cut the square twice diagonally to yield 4 triangles.
- From the fabric for D, cut 1 square, 4½" x 4½".
- From the fabric for E, cut 4 squares, each 4½" x 4½".

Piecing

1. Stitch a triangle A to a triangle B and another triangle A to a triangle C along the short sides to make side-by-side units as shown. Press.

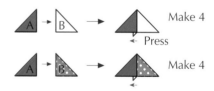

2. Arrange the side-by-side units and stitch together to make 4 squares, each 4½" x 4½". Press in either direction.

Make 4

3. Referring to the block plan, arrange the squares completed in step 2 with squares D and E.

Sew the squares together into 3 rows of 3 squares each. Press. Sew the rows together. Press.

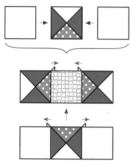

4. To assemble your quilt, refer to "Settings," beginning on page 70.

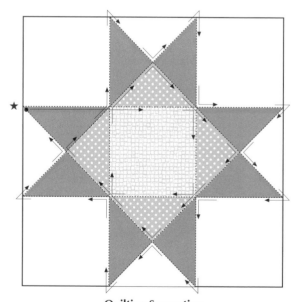

Quilting Suggestion
Arrows indicate stitching direction. See page 80.

Card Trick

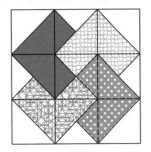
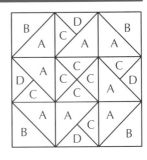

Cutting

- From each of the 4 different fabrics for A, cut 1 square, 4⅞" x 4⅞".
  Cut each square once diagonally to yield 8 triangles.
- From the fabric for B, cut 2 squares, each 4⅞" x 4⅞".
  Cut each square once diagonally to yield 4 triangles.
- From each of the 4 different fabrics for C, cut 1 square, 3¹¹⁄₁₆" x 3¹¹⁄₁₆" (between 3⅝" and 3¾").
  Cut each square once diagonally to yield 8 triangles.
- From the fabric for D, cut 1 square, 5¼" x 5¼".
  Cut the square twice diagonally to yield 4 triangles.

Piecing

1. Stitch 1 triangle A from each of the 4 different fabrics to a triangle B to make 4 different half-square triangle units, each 4½" x 4½". Press toward triangle B.

2. Stitch 1 triangle C from each of the 4 different fabrics to a triangle D on the short sides to make 4 side-by-side units as shown. The short sides of the resulting units should measure 4⅞". Press toward triangle C.

Pay careful attention to the arrangement of your fabrics while doing the next steps.

3. Arrange the remaining 4 different C triangles to form the center square of the block. Stitch 2 C triangles together on the short sides to make a side-by-side unit. Repeat with the other 2 C triangles. Press the seams in opposite directions. Sew the 2 side-by-side units together to make a square, 4½" x 4½". Press.

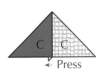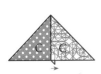

4. Arrange the units and the remaining triangles as shown. Sew the side-by-side units made in step 2 to A triangles to make 4 squares, each 4½" x 4½". Press toward the A triangles. Sew the squares together in 3 rows of 3 squares each. Press the top and bottom seams toward the center square, and the seams in the center row toward the outer squares. Sew the 3 rows together. Press away from the center row.

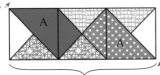

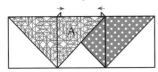

5. To assemble your quilt, refer to "Settings," beginning on page 70.

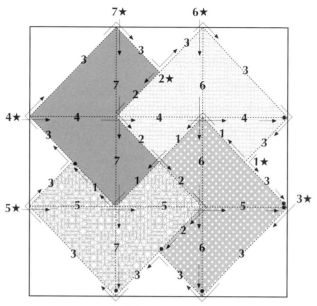

Quilting Suggestion
Arrows and numbers indicate stitching direction and order. See page 80.

Half-Square Triangle Units

A common unit in quiltmaking, half-square triangle units are made by stitching two identical right triangles together along their long sides to create a square. These can be found in the Card Trick, Our Galaxy, and Tall Ship blocks. After sewing, press according to the block directions and then trim away the seam-allowance tips that extend beyond the block edges.

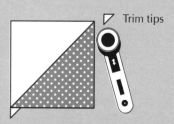

⊿ Trim tips

When you need many identical half-square triangles, you can use the following fast piecing method. This method is used in the blocks Rocky Mountain Puzzle, Prairie Queen, Checkered Heart, Peace and Plenty, Diamond Star, Summer's Dream, Sailboat, Hanging Basket, and Rocking Horse.

1. Following the block directions, cut squares or rectangles. Using your C-Thru ruler, draw a grid on the wrong side of the fabric square or rectangle.

(*Hint:* If the fabric is dark or has a busy print, draw the grid on the fabric that will be used for the other half of the unit.) The grid layout is determined by the number of half-square triangle units required for the block. A square with 1 diagonal line yields 2 half-square triangle units. A rectangle with a grid containing 3 squares that are bisected once diagonally yields 6 half-square triangle units.

2. Place the fabric with the drawn grid on top of the other fabric, right sides together. Make sure to align all raw edges. (If they don't line up exactly, you have probably cut them wrong.) Sew the pieces together, ¼" away from the diagonal lines on both sides. If you don't have a ¼" presser foot, you may draw the seam lines onto the fabric with the C-Thru ruler and sew on the drawn lines.

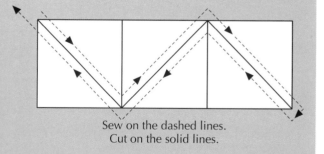

Sew on the dashed lines.
Cut on the solid lines.

3. Cut on all the drawn lines, except the ones that you stitched on. Cut the vertical and horizontal lines accurately; otherwise the size of the half-square triangle units will be incorrect. Press according to the block instructions. In most cases, the pressing is not determined by the lightest or darkest fabric in the unit, but by the direction that will create the flattest seams when the entire block is completed. Trim the seam-allowance tips as shown on page 26. The half-square triangle units are now ready to be sewn into blocks.

Rocky Mountain Puzzle

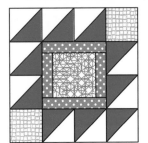 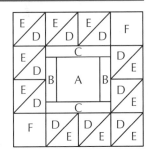

Cutting

- From the fabric for A, cut 1 square, 4½" x 4½".
- From the fabric for B, cut 2 rectangles, each 1½" x 4½".
- From the fabric for C, cut 2 rectangles, each 1½" x 6½".
- From the fabric for D, cut 5 squares, each 3⅞" x 3⅞".
- From the fabric for E, cut 5 squares, each 3⅞" x 3⅞".
- From the fabric for F, cut 2 squares, each 3½" x 3½".

Piecing

1. Stitch a rectangle B to 2 opposite sides of square A. Press toward the rectangles. Then stitch a rectangle C to the top and bottom of square A. Press toward the rectangles.

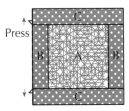

2. Draw a diagonal line on the wrong side of each square E. Refer to "Half-Square Triangle Units" on page 26. With right sides together, stitch squares D and E together on each side of the diagonal line. Cut apart to make 10 half-square triangle units, each 3½" x 3½". Press toward triangle D.

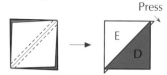

3. Stitch pairs of half-square triangle units together to make 4 strips, each 3½" x 6½", as shown. Press toward triangle E. Note the difference in color location and seam angle.

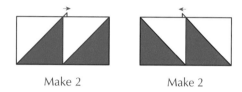

Make 2   Make 2

4. Referring to the block plan, sew the units and F squares together into 3 rows of 3 units each.

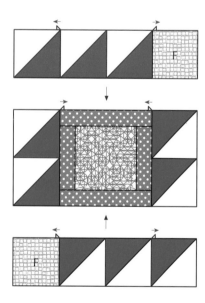

5. Stitch the rows together. Press.

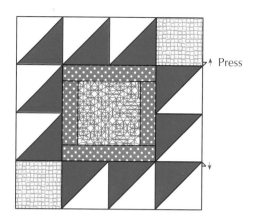

6. To assemble your quilt, refer to "Settings," beginning on page 70.

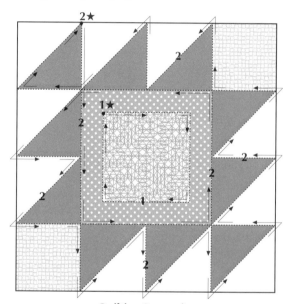

Quilting Suggestion
Arrows and numbers indicate stitching direction and order. See page 80.

Prairie Queen

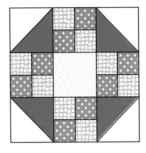

Cutting

- From the fabric for A, cut 1 rectangle, 4⅞" x 9¾".
- From the fabric for B, cut 1 rectangle, 4⅞" x 9¾".
- From the fabric for C, cut 1 strip, 2½" x 22".
- From the fabric for D, cut 1 strip, 2½" x 22".
- From the fabric for E, cut 1 square, 4½" x 4½".

Piecing

1. Draw a grid on the wrong side of rectangle B. Refer to "Half-Square Triangle Units" on page 26. The grid will have 2 squares, each 4⅞" x 4⅞". Draw 1 diagonal line on each square as shown.

2. With right sides facing, stitch rectangles A and B together on each side of the diagonal lines. Cut apart to make 4 half-square triangle units, each 4½" x 4½". Press toward triangle A. Trim seam-allowance tips.

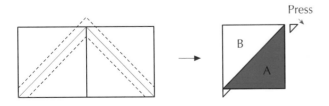

3. Sew strips C and D together along the long edges and press toward the darker fabric. Crosscut into 8 segments, each 2½" x 4½". Stitch pairs of segments together as shown to make four-patch units, each 4½" x 4½". Press in either direction.

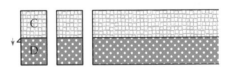

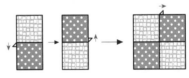

Make 4

4. Referring to the block plan, arrange the half-square triangle units, the E square, and four-patch units. Sew the squares together into 3 rows of 3 squares each. Press.

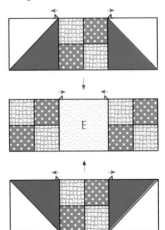

5. Sew the rows together. Press.

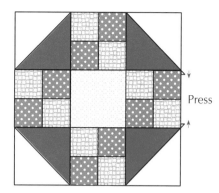

Press

6. To assemble your quilt, refer to "Settings," beginning on page 70.

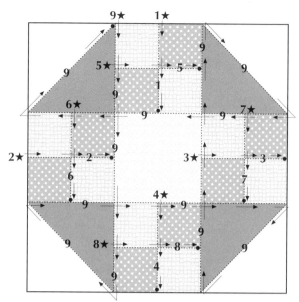

Quilting Suggestion
Arrows and numbers indicate stitching direction and order. See page 80.

Our Galaxy

(a variation of Milky Way)

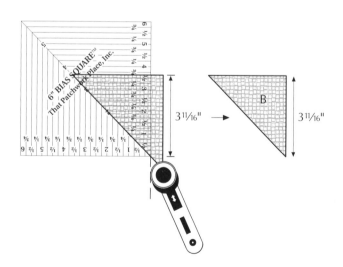

Cutting

- From each of the 4 different fabrics for A, cut 1 square, 4⅞" x 4⅞".
  Cut each square once diagonally to yield 8 triangles.
- To make triangle B, use a Bias Square to trim 1 of each different triangle A so that the short sides measure 3¹¹⁄₁₆" (between 3⅝" and 3¾").
- From each of the 4 different fabrics for C, cut 1 rectangle, 2½" x 5".
- From the fabric for D, cut 2 squares, each 4⅞" x 4⅞".
  Cut each square once diagonally to yield 4 triangles.
- From the fabric for E, cut 4 rectangles, each 2½" x 5".

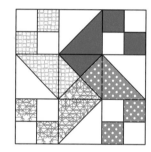

Piecing

1. Arrange B triangles, carefully making sure that you are pleased with the placement of the fabrics. Stitch 2 B triangles together to make a side-by-side unit. Press as shown. Repeat with the remaining 2 B triangles. Sew the 2 side-by-side units together to make 1 square, 4½" x 4½". Press.

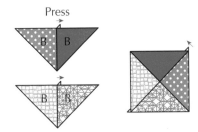

2. Stitch 1 triangle A to each triangle D along the long sides to make 4 half-square triangle units, each 4½" x 4½". Press toward triangle A.

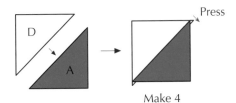

Make 4

3. Sew 1 rectangle E to each rectangle C along the long sides. Press toward the darker fabric. Crosscut into segments, each 2½" x 4½". Stitch 2 segments together to make 1 four-patch unit, 4½" x 4½". Press in either direction.

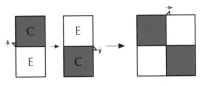

Make 4

4. Referring to the block plan, arrange the units. Sew them together into 3 rows of

3 squares each. Press.

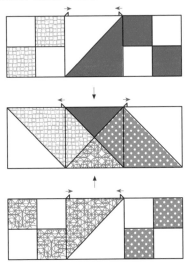

5. Sew the rows together. Press.

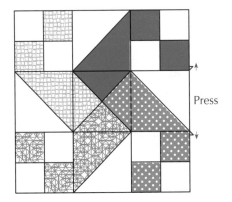

6. To assemble your quilt, refer to "Settings," beginning on page 70.

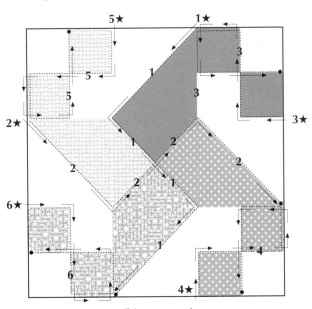

Quilting Suggestion
Arrows and numbers indicate stitching
direction and order. See page 80.

Checkered Heart

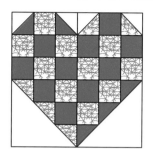
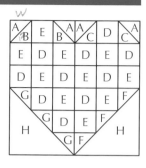

Cutting

white ✓ • From the fabric for A, cut 2 squares, each 2⅞" x 2⅞".
Print ✓ • From the fabric for B, cut 1 square, 2⅞" x 2⅞".
Pink ✓ • From the fabric for C, cut 1 square, 2⅞" x 2⅞".
Print • From the fabric for D, cut 1 strip, 2½" x 27".
Pink • From the fabric for E, cut 1 strip, 2½" x 27".
Print • From the fabric for F, cut 2 squares, each 2⅞" x 2⅞".
  Cut each square once diagonally to yield 4 triangles.
  You will use 3 and have 1 left over.
Pink • From the fabric for G, cut 2 squares, each 2⅞" x 2⅞".
  Cut each square once diagonally to yield 4 triangles.
  You will use 3 and have 1 left over.
white • From the fabric for H, cut 1 square, 6⅞" x 6⅞". Cut the
  square once diagonally to yield 2 triangles.

Piecing

1. Draw a diagonal line on the wrong sides of each square A. Refer to "Half-Square Triangle Units" on page 26. With right sides facing, stitch 1 square A and 1 square B together on each side of the diagonal line. Stitch the remaining square A to square C in the same manner. Cut the units apart to make 4 half-square triangle units, each 2½" x 2½". Press toward triangles B and C.

2. Cut 2 squares, each 2½" x 2½", from strip D and 2 from strip E; set aside.

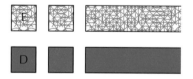

3. Sew the remaining portion of strips D and E together along the long edges. Press toward strip E. Crosscut into 8 segments, each 2½" x 4½".

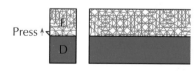

4. Arrange 6 of the segments, the half-square triangle units, 1 square D, and 1 square E as shown. Stitch together in rows. Press. Stitch the rows to make 2 squares, each 6½" x 6½". Press. Sew the squares together as shown and press to make the top half of the heart.

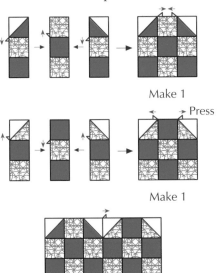

Make 1

Press

Make 1

5. Stitch 1 of the remaining segments to a triangle G. Press toward the triangle. Stitch a triangle G to 2 sides of the remaining square D as shown. Press toward the triangles.
(*Hint:* Match the corners of the triangles with the corners of the squares. The tips of the triangles extend beyond the edges of the squares.) Stitch the resulting 2 units together to make a triangle measuring 6⅞" on each short side. Press.

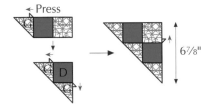

6. Stitch the last segment to a triangle F. Press toward the segment. Stitch a triangle F to 2 sides of the remaining square E. Press toward the triangles. (Refer to the hint in step 5 above.) Stitch the resulting 2 units together to make a triangle measuring 6⅞" on each short side. Press.

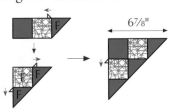

7. Sew each triangle from steps 5 and 6 to a triangle H to make 2 squares, each 6½" x 6½". Press toward triangle H. Sew the squares together as shown and press to make the bottom half of the heart.

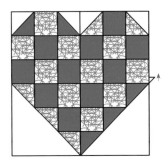

8. Sew the top and bottom halves of the heart together and press to complete the block.

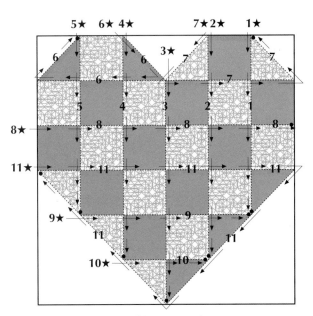

9. To assemble your quilt, refer to "Settings," beginning on page 70.

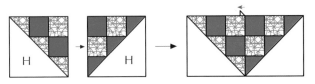

Quilting Suggestion
Arrows and numbers indicate stitching direction and order. See page 80.

Trapezoids

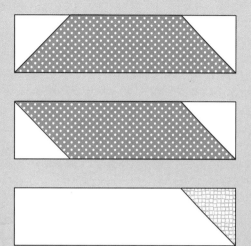

By trimming rectangles to make trapezoids or parallelograms and adding triangles, you can make pieced rectangles. Use these units to make the boat bottoms of the Sailboat (page 35) and Tall Ship (page 36), the sails of the Tall Ship, and the rooftops of the Schoolhouse (page 57) and Saltbox House (page 59). Follow the directions given with each of the blocks to cut the correct angles.

1. With the right side of the fabric facing up, align the diagonal line on your Bias Square with the bottom long edge of the fabric rectangle. Align the edge of the ruler that you will cut against with the top corner of the fabric rectangle. Cut.

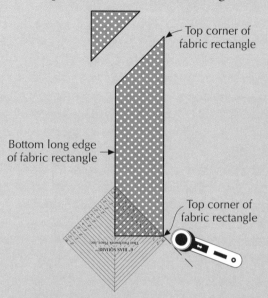

Top corner of fabric rectangle

Bottom long edge of fabric rectangle

Top corner of fabric rectangle

2. With right sides together, align the long side of a triangle with each short edge of a trapezoid as shown. One tip of the triangle will align with the tip of the trapezoid, and the other triangle tip will extend beyond the trapezoid. Sew. Press.

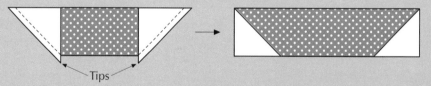

Tips

Sailboat

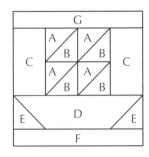

Cutting

- From the fabric for A, cut 1 rectangle, 3⅞" x 7¾".
- From the fabric for B, cut 1 rectangle, 3⅞" x 7¾".
- From the fabric for C, cut 2 rectangles, each 3½" x 6½".
- From the fabric for D, cut 1 rectangle, 3½" x 13¼".
- From the fabric for E, cut 1 square, 3⅞" x 3⅞". Cut the square once diagonally to yield 2 triangles.
- From the fabric for F, cut 1 rectangle, 2" x 12½".
- From the fabric for G, cut 1 rectangle, 2" x 12½".

Piecing

1. Draw a grid on the wrong side of rectangle A. Refer to "Half-Square Triangle Units" on page 26. The grid will have 2 squares, each 3⅞" x 3⅞". Draw 1 diagonal line in each square.

2. With right sides facing, stitch rectangles A and B together on each side of the diagonal lines. Cut apart to make 4 half-square triangle units, each 3½" x 3½". Press toward triangle B. Trim the seam-allowance tips.

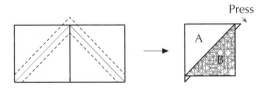

3. Stitch the 4 half-square triangle units together as shown to make 2 rectangles. Press.

4. Before you stitch the rectangles together to make a 6½" x 6½" square, decide which direction you want the sails to point—right or left. In "Ships That Pass in the Night" (page 17), the direction of the sails varies from block to block. Stitch. Press in either direction.

 or

Left   Right

5. Sew a rectangle C to opposite sides of the sails. Press toward rectangle C.

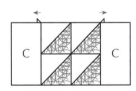

6. Trim rectangle D to make a trapezoid. Refer to "Trapezoids" on page 34. Stitch a triangle E to each end of the trapezoid to make the boat hull and "water." Press toward triangle E.

7. Sew the hull to the sails and press toward the hull. Sew rectangles F and G in place as shown. Press toward rectangles F and G.

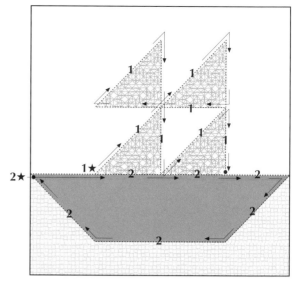

8. To assemble your quilt, refer to "Settings," beginning on page 70.

Quilting Suggestion
Arrows and numbers indicate stitching
direction and order. See page 80.

Tall Ship

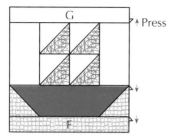

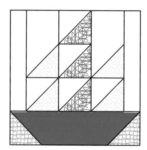

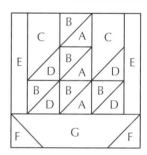

Cutting

- From the fabric for A, cut 2 squares, each 3⅞" x 3⅞". Cut each square once diagonally to yield 4 triangles. You will use 3 and have 1 left over.
- From the fabric for B, cut 3 squares, each 3⅞" x 3⅞". Cut each square once diagonally to yield 6 triangles. You will use 5 and have 1 left over.
- From the fabric for C, cut 2 rectangles, each 3½" x 6⅞".
- From the fabric for D, cut 2 squares, each 3⅞" x 3⅞". Cut each square once diagonally to yield 4 triangles.
- From the fabric for E, cut 2 rectangles, each 2" x 9½".
- From the fabric for F, cut 1 square, 3⅞" x 3⅞". Cut the square once diagonally to yield 2 triangles.
- From the fabric for G, cut 1 rectangle, 3½" x 13¼".

Piecing

1. Stitch a triangle A to a triangle B to make a half-square triangle unit, 3½" x 3½". Stitch a triangle B to a triangle D. Make 3 A/B units and 2 B/D units. Press toward triangles A and D.

Make 3

Make 2

2. Trim the C rectangles to make 2 trapezoids. Refer to "Trapezoids" on page 34. Stitch a triangle D to 1 end of each trapezoid. Press toward the triangles.

Make 2

3. Stitch a half-square triangle unit to each rectangle made in step 2 as shown, to make 2 sail strips. Press toward the half-square triangle units.

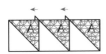

4. Stitch the 3 remaining half-square triangle units together to make the center sail strip. Press.

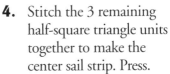

5. Sew the 3 sail strips together and add the E rectangles as shown to make a rectangle, 9½" x 12½". Press.

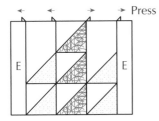

6. Trim rectangle G to make a trapezoid. Stitch a triangle F to each short end of the trapezoid to make the boat hull and "water." Press toward the triangles.

7. Sew the hull to the sails and press toward the hull.

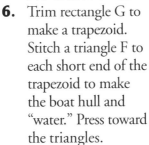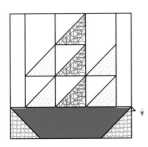

8. To assemble your quilt, refer to "Settings," beginning on page 70.

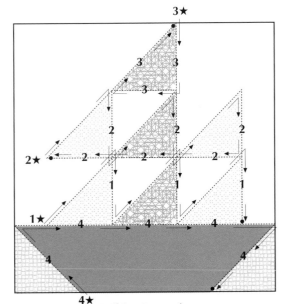

Quilting Suggestion
Arrows and numbers indicate stitching direction and order. See page 80.

Flying Geese Units

Flying Geese units are made up of one large triangle (the goose) and two smaller triangles (the sky). When stitched together, these triangles form a rectangle.

Aligning the long sides of the small triangles with the short sides of the larger center triangle correctly is the key to success. The block directions tell you what size to cut the triangles. Blocks that include this unit are: Mother's Fancy Star, Summer's Dream, Dutchman's Puzzle, Diamond Star, Devil's Claw, Goose on the Loose, and Sailor's Star.

1. Starting with the small triangle on the right-hand side, place it right sides together with the center triangle as shown. Align the long edge of the small triangle with the short edge of the center triangle. The tip of the small triangle extends above the center triangle. Stitch the pieces together. Press the seam away from the center triangle.

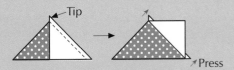

2. Repeat with the left-hand small triangle to complete the unit. Trim the seam-allowance tips that extend beyond the center triangle.

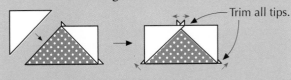

Mother's Fancy Star

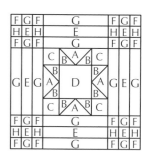

Cutting

- From the fabric for A, cut 1 square, 4¼" x 4¼". Cut the square twice diagonally to yield 4 triangles.
- From the fabric for B, cut 4 squares, each 2⅜" x 2⅜". Cut each square once diagonally to yield 8 triangles.
- From the fabric for C, cut 4 squares, each 2" x 2".
- From the fabric for D, cut 1 square, 3½" x 3½".
- From the fabric for E, cut 1 strip, 1½" x 34".
- From the fabric for F, cut 2 strips, each 1½" x 13".
- From the fabric for G, cut 2 strips, each 1½" x 34".
- From the fabric for H, cut 1 strip, 1½" x 13".

Piecing

1. Stitch triangles A and B together to make 4 Flying Geese units, each 2" x 3½". Refer to "Flying Geese Units" on page 37.

   Make 4

2. Stitch a square C to each side of 2 of the Flying Geese units. Press toward square C.

   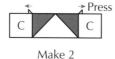

   Make 2

3. Stitch the 2 remaining Flying Geese units to opposite sides of square D. Press toward square D.

   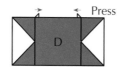

4. Sew the Flying Geese strips created in step 2 to the top and bottom of the unit made in step 3, to make the center star. Press toward square D. The center star should measure 6½" x 6½".

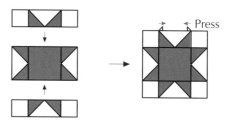

5. Create ninepatch units and sashing units by sewing a strip G to each side of strip E. Press toward the E strip. Sew a strip F to each side of strip H. Press toward the F strips.

   Crosscut the G/E/G strips into 4 segments, each 3½" x 6½", for the sashing units, and 4 segments, each 1½" x 3½", for the ninepatch units.

   Crosscut the F/H/F strips into 8 segments, each 1½" x 3½", for the ninepatch units.

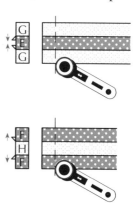

6. Stitch the 1½" x 3½" segments together as shown to make 4 ninepatch units, each 3½" x 3½". Press toward the F/H/F segments.

7. Sew the ninepatch units and 2 sashing units together to make the top and bottom rows of the block. Press toward the sashing units. Sew the remaining 2 sashing units and the center star together as shown to make the center row. Press toward the sashings. Sew the rows together. Press toward the center star.

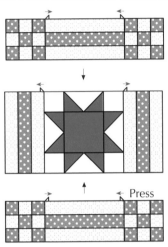

8. To assemble your quilt, refer to "Settings," beginning on page 70.

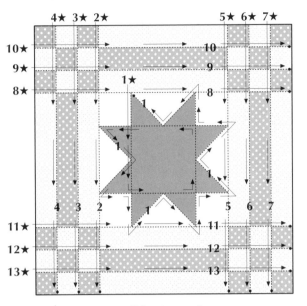

Quilting Suggestion
Arrows and numbers indicate stitching direction and order. See page 80.

Summer's Dream

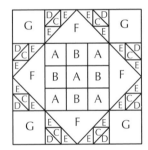

Cutting

- From the fabric for A, cut 5 squares, each 2½" x 2½".
- From the fabric for B, cut 4 squares, each 2½" x 2½".
- From the fabric for C, cut 1 square, 4¾" x 4¾".
- From the fabric for D, cut 1 square, 4¾" x 4¾".
- From the fabric for E, cut 1 strip, 2⅜" x 22"; crosscut into 8 squares, each 2⅜" x 2⅜".
  Cut each square once diagonally to yield 16 triangles.
- From the fabric for F, cut 1 square, 7¼" x 7¼".
  Cut the square twice diagonally to yield 4 triangles.
- From the fabric for G, cut 4 squares, each 3½" x 3½".

Piecing

1. Stitch squares A and B as shown to make a ninepatch unit, 6½" x 6½". Press.

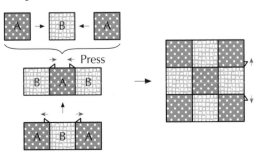

2. Draw a grid on the wrong side of square D. Refer to "Half-Square Triangle Units" on page 26. The grid will have 4 squares, each 2⅜" x 2⅜". Draw 1 diagonal line in each square.

3. With right sides facing, stitch squares C and D together on each side of the diagonal lines. Cut apart to make 8 half-square triangle units, each 2" x 2". Press toward triangle C.

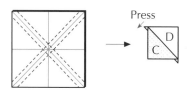

4. Stitch a triangle E to adjacent sides of the half-square triangle units to make 8 triangles that measure 3⅞" on the short sides.

   (*Hint:* Match the corners of the triangles with the corners of the half-square triangle units. The tips of the triangles extend beyond the edges of the half-square triangle units.)

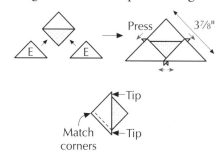

5. Stitch each triangle F to 2 triangles made in step 4, to make 4 rectangles, each 3½" x 6½". Refer to "Flying Geese Units" on page 37.

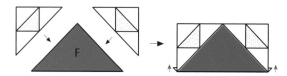

6. Referring to the block plan, sew the units and G squares together into 3 rows of 3 units each. Press.

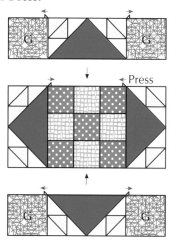

7. Sew the rows together. Press.

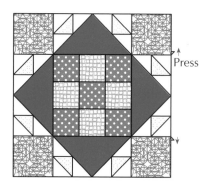

8. To assemble your quilt, refer to "Settings," beginning on page 70.

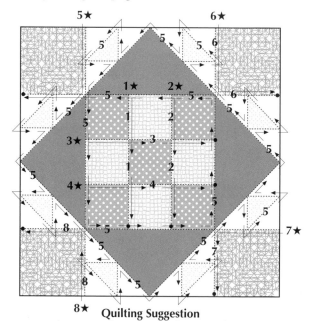

Quilting Suggestion
Arrows and numbers indicate stitching direction and order. See page 80.

Pinwheel Centers

Many of the units and blocks have eight triangles that meet in the center. Dutchman's Puzzle, Diamond Star, Peace and Plenty, Whirling Star, and the Pinwheel corner sashing are places where this occurs. Here is a great pressing technique that eliminates the bulk in the seam allowance and ensures that the points meet and lie flat.

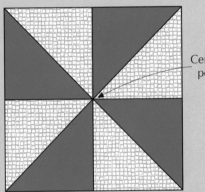

Center where points join

1. The pressing directions for the blocks tell you to press all the seams in a clockwise or counterclockwise fashion. Follow the pressing directions for the block carefully. This trick only works when the unit is pressed correctly.

2. After sewing the last seam, remove the stitches within the seam allowances as shown.

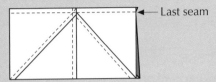

Last seam

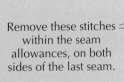

Remove these stitches within the seam allowances, on both sides of the last seam.

3. Press as shown. The seams will swirl in the same direction—either in a clockwise or counterclockwise fashion.

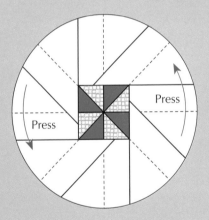

Press

Press

Dutchman's Puzzle

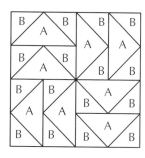

Cutting

- From each of the 4 different fabrics for A, cut 1 square, 5⅛" x 5⅛".
  Cut each square once diagonally to yield 8 triangles.
- From the fabric for B, cut 8 squares, each 3⅞" x 3⅞".
  Cut each square once diagonally to yield 16 triangles.

Piecing

1. Piece the A and B triangles together to make 8 Flying Geese, each 3½" x 6½". Refer to "Flying Geese Units" on page 37. Pair up the Flying Geese by like fabrics and stitch them together to make 4 squares, each 6½" x 6½". Press seam toward triangle A as shown. (*Hint:* Triangles have bias edges, so treat them gently. If you have stretched a bias edge while pressing, in the next assembly step, align the unstretched edge with the next piece. With right sides facing, stitch the pieces together, easing in the stretched edge.)

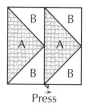

Press

2. Sew the squares together into 2 rows of 2 units each. Sew the 2 rows together. Press, referring to "Pinwheel Centers" on page 41.

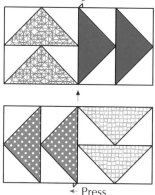

← Press

3. To assemble your quilt, refer to "Settings," beginning on page 70.

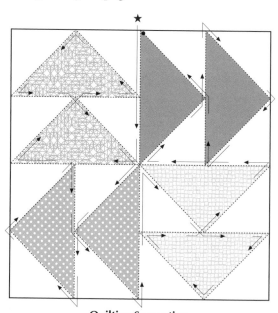

Quilting Suggestion
Arrows indicate stitching direction. See page 80.

Diamond Star

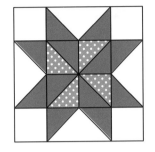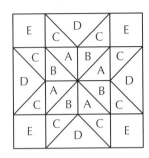

Cutting

- From the fabric for A, cut 1 rectangle, 3⅞" x 7¾".
- From the fabric for B, cut 1 rectangle, 3⅞" x 7¾".
- From the fabric for C, cut 4 squares, each 3⅞" x 3⅞".
  Cut each square once diagonally to yield 8 triangles.
- From the fabric for D, cut 1 square, 7¼" x 7¼".
  Cut the square twice diagonally to yield 4 triangles.
- From the fabric for E, cut 4 squares, each 3½" x 3½".

Piecing

1. Draw a grid on the wrong side of rectangle B. Refer to "Half-Square Triangle Units" on page 26. The grid will have 2 squares, each 3⅞" x 3⅞". Draw 1 diagonal line in each square.

2. With right sides facing, stitch rectangles A and B together on each side of the diagonal lines. Cut apart to make 4 half-square triangle units, each 3½" x 3½". Press toward triangle A.

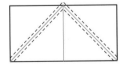

3. Stitch the half-square triangle units together in pairs as shown to make 2 rectangles, each 3½" x 6½". Press.

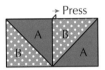

Make 2

4. Stitch the 2 rectangles together to make a square, 6½" x 6½". Press the seams, referring to "Pinwheel Centers" on page 41.

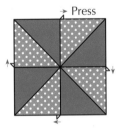

5. Stitch triangles C and D together to make 4 Flying Geese units, each 3½" x 6½". Press. Refer to "Flying Geese Units" on page 37.

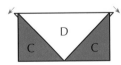

6. Referring to the block plan, stitch the units together into 3 rows.

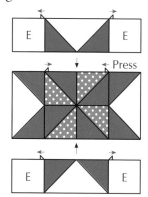

7. Stitch the rows together. Press.

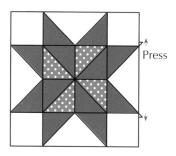

8. To assemble your quilt, refer to "Settings," beginning on page 70.

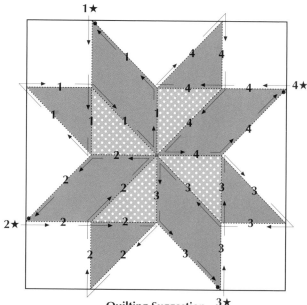

Quilting Suggestion
Arrows and numbers indicate stitching direction and order. See page 80.

Peace and Plenty

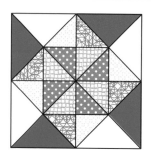 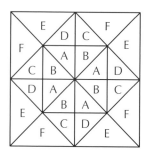

Cutting

- From the fabric for A, cut 1 rectangle, 3⅞" x 7¾".
- From the fabric for B, cut 1 rectangle, 3⅞" x 7¾".
- From the fabric for C, cut 2 squares, each 3⅞" x 3⅞".
  Cut each square once diagonally to yield 4 triangles.
- From the fabric for D, cut 2 squares, each 3⅞" x 3⅞".
  Cut each square once diagonally to yield 4 triangles.
- From the fabric for E, cut 1 square, 7¼" x 7¼".
  Cut the square twice diagonally to yield 4 triangles.
- From the fabric for F, cut 1 square, 7¼" x 7¼".
  Cut the square twice diagonally to yield 4 triangles.

Piecing

1. Draw a grid on the wrong side of rectangle A. Refer to "Half-Square Triangle Units" on page 26. The grid will have 2 squares, each 3⅞" x 3⅞. Draw 1 diagonal line in each square.

2. With right sides facing, stitch rectangles A and B together on each side of the diagonal line. Cut the units apart to make 4 half-square triangle units. Press toward triangle A.

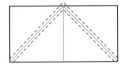

3. Stitch triangles C and D to each side of the 4 half-square triangle units to make 4 pieced triangles, each measuring 6⅞" on the short sides. Press toward triangles C and D. (*Hint:* Align the corners of the triangles with the corners of the half-square triangle units. The tips of the triangles will extend beyond the edges of the half-square triangle units.)

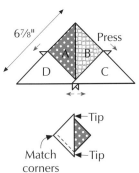

4. Stitch triangles E and F together along the short sides to make 4 side-by-side triangle units. Press toward triangle F. The short sides of the side-by-side units should measure 6⅞".

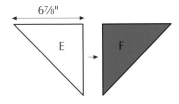

5. Arrange the triangle units made in steps 3 and 4 as shown. Sew together along the long sides to make 4 squares, each 6½" x 6½". Press.

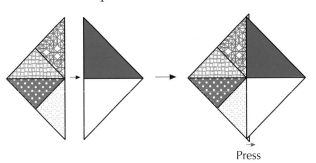

6. Referring to the block plan, sew the 4 squares together. Press, referring to "Pinwheel Centers" on page 41.

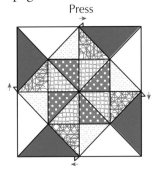

7. To assemble your quilt, refer to "Settings," beginning on page 70.

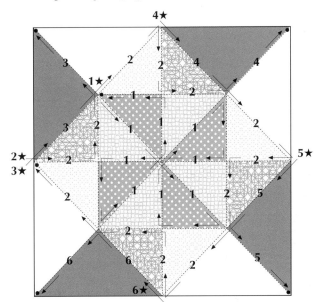

Quilting Suggestion
Arrows and numbers indicate stitching direction and order. See page 80.

Square-in-a-Square Units

These units are formed when four triangles surround a center square to form a larger square. Matching up edges, points, and seams will help keep your block square. *Always* press toward the triangles. Blocks that contain these units are: Devil's Claw, Windblown Square, Goose on the Loose, Snail's Trail, and Sailor's Star.

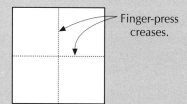

1. To help align the triangles accurately, fold the center square in half in both directions and finger-press.

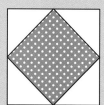

Finger-press creases.

2. With right sides together, place the long side of one of the triangles on one side of the square. Make sure the raw edges of the two pieces of fabric are even and the corner of the triangle is aligned with

a creased line as shown. The other two corners (tips) of the triangle will extend beyond the edges of the square. Stitch the pieces together.

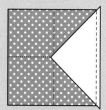

3. Press the seam away from the center square. Repeat the process by stitching a triangle to the opposite side of the square.

Press

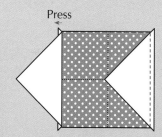

4. Stitch the remaining two triangles to the other sides of the square. Trim the seam-allowance tips.

Trim tips

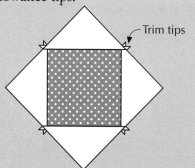

Devil's Claw

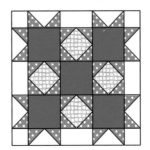 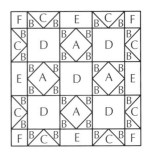

Cutting

- From the fabric for A, cut 4 squares, each 2⅝" x 2⅝".
- From the fabric for B, cut 1 strip, 2⅜" x 42"; crosscut into 16 squares, each 2⅜" x 2⅜".
  Cut each square once diagonally to yield 32 triangles.
- From the fabric for C, cut 2 squares, each 4¼" x 4¼".
  Cut each square twice diagonally to yield 8 triangles.
- From the fabric for D, cut 5 squares, each 3½" x 3½".
- From the fabric for E, cut 4 rectangles, each 2" x 3½".
- From the fabric for F, cut 4 squares, each 2" x 2".

Piecing

1. Stitch a triangle B to the sides of each square A to make 4 square-in-a-square units, each 3½" x 3½". Refer to "Square-in-a-Square Units" on page 46.

2. Stitch 2 B triangles to each triangle C to make 8 Flying Geese units, each 2" x 3½". Refer to "Flying Geese Units" on page 37.

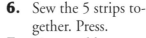

3. Make 2 strips, each including 2 Flying Geese units, 2 F squares, and 1 rectangle E. Press.

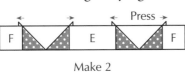

Make 2

4. Make 2 strips, each including 2 Flying Geese units, 2 D squares, and 1 square-in-a-square unit. Press.

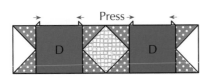

Make 2

5. Make 1 center strip, including the remaining 2 E rectangles, the remaining square D, and the remaining 2 square-in-a-square units. Press.

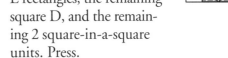

Make 1

6. Sew the 5 strips together. Press.

7. To assemble your quilt, refer to "Settings," beginning on page 70.

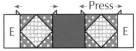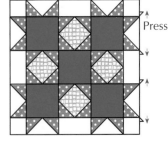

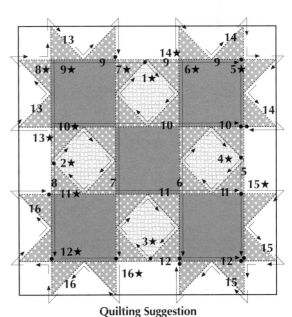

Quilting Suggestion
Arrows and numbers indicate stitching direction and order. See page 80.

Snail's Trail

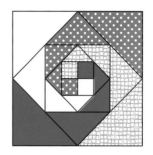
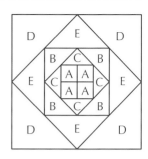

Cutting

- From each of the 4 different fabrics for A, cut 1 square, 2" x 2".
- From each of the 4 different fabrics for B, cut 1 square, 3⅞" x 3⅞".
  Cut each square once diagonally to yield 8 triangles.
- To make the C triangles, use a Bias Square to trim 1 of each different triangle B so that the short sides measure 3".

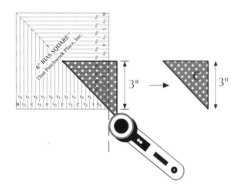

- From each of the 4 different fabrics for D, cut 1 square, 6⅞" x 6⅞".
  Cut each square once diagonally to yield 8 triangles.
- To make E triangles, use a Bias Square to trim 1 of each different triangle D so that the short sides measure 5⅛".

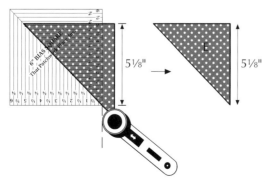

Piecing

1. Stitch the 4 A squares together as shown to make a four-patch unit, 3½" x 3½". Press. Be sure that the placement of the fabrics is correct because it will affect the rest of the block.

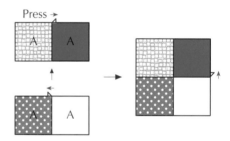

2. Stitch the C triangles to the four-patch unit to make a square measuring 4¾" x 4¾". Refer to "Square-in-a-Square Units" on page 46. In this block, however, sew the triangles to adjacent sides of the square rather than to opposite sides. Be sure your fabrics are placed correctly. Press toward the just-added triangle after each seam is stitched.

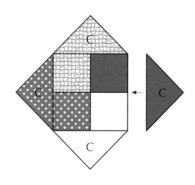

3. Sew the remaining 4 B triangles to the square made in step 2, following the same procedure as before. The resulting square should now measure 6½" x 6½". Press as before.

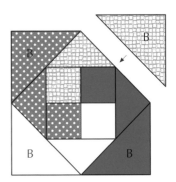

4. Stitch the remaining E triangles to the square made in step 3, following the same procedure as before. The resulting square should now measure 9" x 9". Press as before.

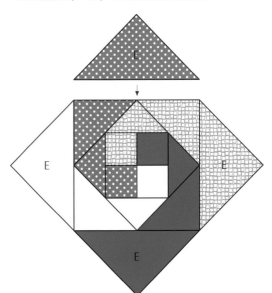

5. Following the same procedure, sew the 4 D triangles to the square made in step 4, to complete the block. Press as before.

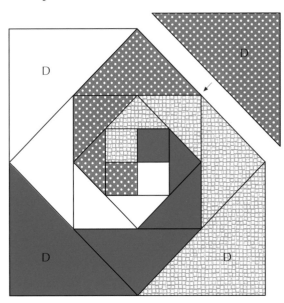

6. To assemble your quilt, refer to "Settings," beginning on page 70.

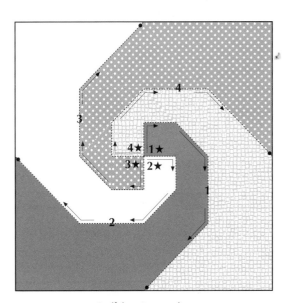

Quilting Suggestion
Arrows and numbers indicate stitching direction and order. See page 80.

Windblown Square

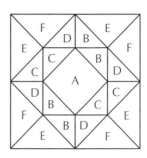

Cutting

- From the fabric for A, cut 1 square, 4¾" x 4¾".
- From the fabric for B, cut 2 squares, each 3⅞" x 3⅞".
  Cut each square once diagonally to yield 4 triangles.
- From the fabric for C, cut 2 squares, each 3⅞" x 3⅞".
  Cut each square once diagonally to yield 4 triangles.
- From the fabric for D, cut 2 squares, each 3⅞" x 3⅞".
  Cut each square once diagonally to yield 4 triangles.
- From the fabric for E, cut 1 square, 7¼" x 7¼".
  Cut the square twice diagonally to yield 4 triangles.
- From the fabric for F, cut 1 square, 7¼" x 7¼".
  Cut the square twice diagonally to yield 4 triangles.

Piecing

1. Stitch 2 B triangles and 2 C triangles to square A as shown to make a square-in-a-square, 6½" x 6½". Refer to "Square-in-a-Square Units" on page 46.

2. Stitch the remaining B and C triangles to the D triangles to make 4 triangles as shown. The short sides should measure 5⅛". Press toward triangles B and C.

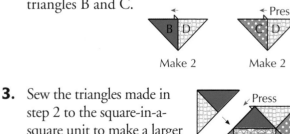

Make 2   Make 2

3. Sew the triangles made in step 2 to the square-in-a-square unit to make a larger square-in-a-square, now measuring 9" x 9". Press away from the triangles.

Press

4. Stitch triangles E and F together to make pieced triangles, with short sides measuring 6⅞". Press toward triangle F.

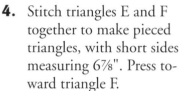

Press

5. Sew the triangles made in step 4 to the large square-in-a-square, following the same procedure as in step 3. Press toward the triangles.

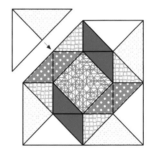

6. To assemble your quilt, refer to "Settings," beginning on page 70.

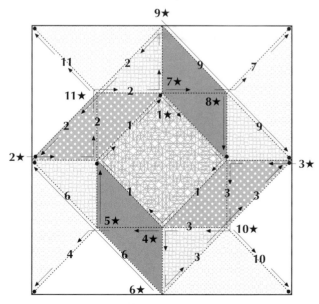

Quilting Suggestion
Arrows and numbers indicate stitching direction and order. See page 80.

Goose on the Loose

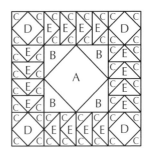

Cutting

- From the fabric for A, cut 1 square, 4¾" x 4¾".
- From the fabric for B, cut 2 squares, each 3⅞" x 3⅞".
  Cut each square once diagonally to yield 4 triangles.
- From the fabric for C, cut 2 strips, 2⅜" x 30"; crosscut into 24 squares, each 2⅜" x 2⅜".
  Cut each square once diagonally to yield 48 triangles.
- From each of 4 different fabrics for D, cut 1 square, 2⅝" x 2⅝".
- From each of 4 different fabrics for E, cut 1 square, 4¼" x 4¼".
  Cut each square twice diagonally to yield 16 triangles.

Piecing

1. Stitch the B triangles to the sides of square A to make 1 square-in-a-square, 6½" x 6½". Refer to "Square-in-a-Square Units" on page 46.

2. Sew 4 C triangles to the sides of each square D to make 4 square-in-a-square units, each 3½" x 3½".

3. Stitch 2 C triangles to each triangle E to make 16 Flying Geese units, each 2" x 3½". Refer to "Flying Geese Units" on page 37. Sew units together into 4 strips of 4 units each as shown. Press toward the "points."

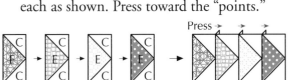

4. Referring to the block plan, arrange the units. Sew the units together to make 3 rows. Sew the rows together. Press.

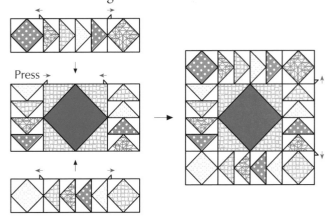

5. To assemble your quilt, refer to "Settings," beginning on page 70.

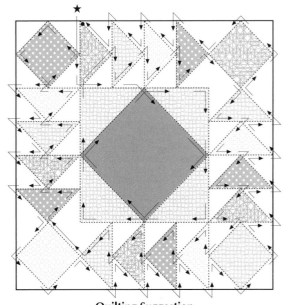

Quilting Suggestion
Arrows indicate stitching direction. See page 80.

Album

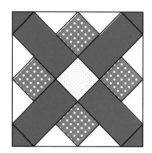

Cutting

- From the fabric for A, cut 4 rectangles, each 3⅝₆" x 6¾₆".
  (If your ruler does not have ¼₆" increments, ⅝₆" is
  between ¼" and ⅜"; ¾₆ is between ⅛" and ¼".)
- From the fabric for B, cut 2 squares, each 2⅞" x 2⅞".
  Cut each square once diagonally to yield 4 triangles.
- From the fabric for C, cut 4 squares, each 3⅝₆" x 3⅝₆".
- From the fabric for D, cut 2 squares, each 5¼" x 5¼".
  Cut each square twice diagonally to yield 8 triangles.
- From the fabric for E, cut 1 square, 3⅝₆" x 3⅝₆".

Piecing

1. Stitch a triangle B to one end of each rect-
    angle A. The point of B should align with the
    center of the rectangle. Finger-press a crease
    in the rectangles and use the crease to align
    the triangles. Press toward the triangles.

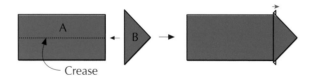

2. Stitch 2 D triangles to each square C to
    make 4 triangles that measure 6⅝₆" on the
    short sides.
    (*Hint:* Match the corner of the triangle with
    the corner of the square as shown. The tips of

the triangle will extend beyond the edges of
the square.) Press toward triangle D.

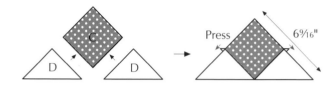

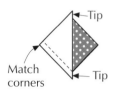

3. Stitch a triangle made in step 2 to each side
    of 2 of the units made in step 1. Follow the
    hint in step 2 to match the corners of the tri-
    angles with the corners of the rectangles. Press.

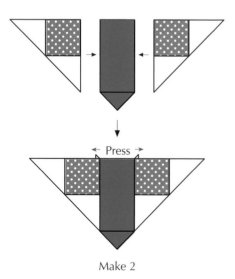

Make 2

4. Sew the remaining 2 units made in step 1 to opposite sides of square E to make a strip. Press toward square E.

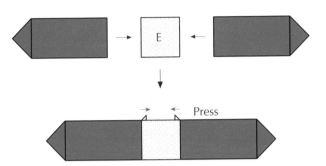

Press

5. Sew the units made in step 3 to both sides of the strip made in step 4. Match the center seams to align the blocks. Press toward the triangles.

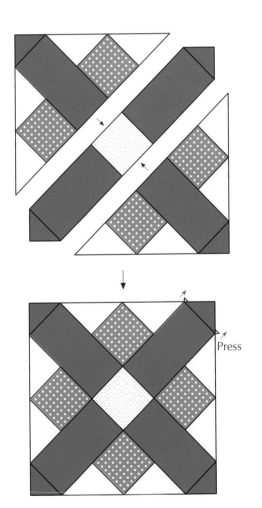

Press

6. To assemble your quilt, refer to "Settings," beginning on page 70.

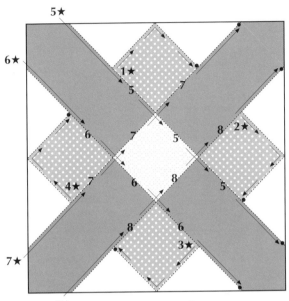

Quilting Suggestion
Arrows and numbers indicate stitching direction and order. See page 80.

Sailor's Star

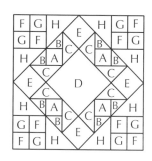

Cutting

- From the fabric for A, cut 4 squares, each 2" x 2".
- From the fabric for B, cut 2 squares, each 3⅜" x 3⅜".
  Cut each square twice diagonally to yield 8 triangles.
- From the fabric for C, cut 4 squares, each 3" x 3".
  Cut each square once diagonally to yield 8 triangles.
- From the fabric for D, cut 1 square, 4¾" x 4¾".
- From the fabric for E, cut 4 squares, each 2⅝" x 2⅝".
- From the fabric for F, cut 1 strip, 2" x 18".
- From the fabric for G, cut 1 strip, 2" x 18".
- From the fabric for H, cut 4 squares, each 3⅞" x 3⅞".
  Cut each square once diagonally to yield 8 triangles.

Piecing

1. Stitch 2 B triangles to each square A to make 4 pieced triangles that measure 3⅞" on the short sides. (*Hint*: Match the corner of the triangle with the corner of the square. The tips of the triangle will extend beyond the edges of the square.) Press toward the triangles.

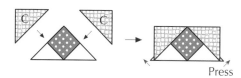

2. Stitch 2 C triangles to each triangle made in step 1, to make 4 Flying Geese units, each 2⅝" x 4¾". Refer to "Flying Geese Units" on page 37. Press.

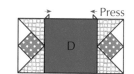

3. Sew 2 of the Flying Geese units to opposite sides of square D. Press toward square D.

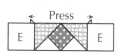

4. Stitch a square E to the short sides of the remaining 2 Flying Geese units. Press toward square E.

5. Sew the strips made in steps 3 and 4 together, to make a larger square, 9" x 9". Press toward the center strip.

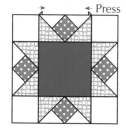

6. Sew strips F and G together on the long sides. Press toward the darker fabric. Crosscut into 8 segments, each 2" x 3½". Stitch the segments together to make 4 four-patch units, each 3½" x 3½". Press in either direction.

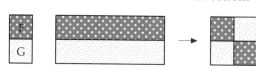

7. Sew 2 H triangles to each four-patch unit as shown to make 4 pieced triangles that measure 6⅞" on the short sides. Press toward triangle H. Refer to the hint in step 1.

8. Sew the triangles made in step 7 to the square made in step 5, to complete the block. Press toward the triangles.

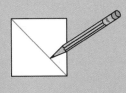

9. To assemble your quilt, refer to "Settings," beginning on page 70.

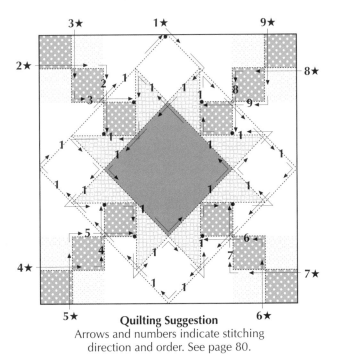

Quilting Suggestion
Arrows and numbers indicate stitching direction and order. See page 80.

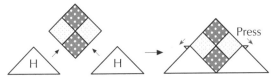

Cut Corners

Cut corners are used in some of the blocks in this book, such as in the Bow Ties, Schoolhouse, Saltbox House, Hanging Basket, Whirling Star, and Rocking Horse. This nifty trick eliminates extra seams and quickly and accurately adds a contrasting corner to a rectangle, square, or triangle.

1. For example, cut a 3½" square from one fabric and a 2" square from another fabric. On the wrong side of the 2" square, draw a diagonal line. (The illustrations in the directions for the blocks always show the fabric with the wrong side up.)

2. With right sides together, place the 2" square on the corner of the 3½" square, aligning the outside edges. Stitch on the diagonal line. Trim away the excess fabric, ¼" away from the seam. Press toward the resulting triangle.

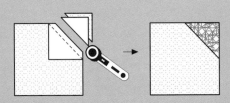

Bow Ties

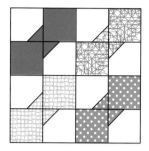

Cutting

- From the fabric for A, cut 8 squares, each 3½" x 3½".
- From each of the 4 different fabrics for B and C, cut:
  2 squares, each 2" x 2", for B
  2 squares, each 3½" x 3½", for C

Piecing

1. Draw 1 diagonal line on the wrong side of each square B. With right sides facing, stitch squares A and B together on the diagonal line. Refer to "Cut Corners" on page 55. Trim away excess fabric to make 8 cut-corner squares, each 3½" x 3½". Press toward triangle B.

2. Matching like fabrics, stitch each square C to a cut-corner square, to make 8 rectangles, each 3½" x 6½". Press toward square C.

3. Pair up the rectangles, matching like fabrics. Align edges and seams. Stitch the pairs together to make 4 squares, each 6½" x 6½". Sew the squares together into 2 rows of 2 blocks each. Press as shown.

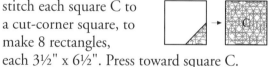

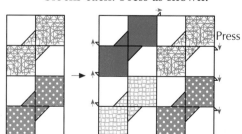

4. Sew the rows together. Press.
5. To assemble your quilt, refer to "Settings," beginning on page 70.

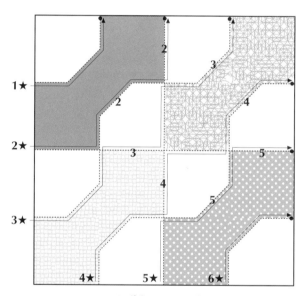

Quilting Suggestion
Arrows and numbers indicate stitching direction and order. See page 80.

Tip

The Schoolhouse, Saltbox House, and Hanging Basket blocks (pages 57–63) are fun to make and are especially good for adding a bit of your personality. Landscape the house with flowers in the "front yard" or add flowers or fruit to the basket.

Schoolhouse

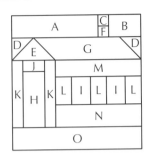

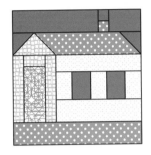

Cutting

- From the fabric for A, cut 1 rectangle, 2½" x 8½", for sky.
- From the fabric for B, cut 1 rectangle, 2½" x 3½", for sky.
- From the fabric for C, cut 1 square, 1½" x 1½", for sky.
- From the fabric for D, cut 1 square, 2⅞" x 2⅞". Cut the square once diagonally to yield 2 triangles for sky.
- From the fabric for E, cut 1 rectangle, 2½" x 4⅞", for roof.
- From the fabric for F, cut 1 square, 1½" x 1½", for chimney.
- From the fabric for G, cut 1 rectangle, 2½" x 11¼", for roof.
- From the fabric for H, cut 1 rectangle, 2½" x 5½", for door.
- From the fabric for I, cut 2 rectangles, each 2¼" x 3", for windows.
- From the fabric for J, cut 1 rectangle, 1½" x 2½", for door wall.
- From the fabric for K, cut 2 rectangles, each 1½" x 6½", for door wall.
- From the fabric for L, cut 3 rectangles, each 2" x 3", for window wall.
- From the fabric for M, cut 1 rectangle, 2" x 8½", for window wall.
- From the fabric for N, cut 1 rectangle, 2½" x 8½", for window wall.
- From the fabric for O, cut 1 rectangle, 2½" x 12½", for grass.

Piecing

1. Stitch squares C and F together. Press toward square C. Stitch rectangles A and B in place as shown to complete the sky/chimney unit. Press.

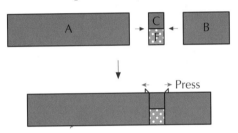

2. Trim rectangle E to make a trapezoid. Refer to "Trapezoids" on page 34. Stitch the long side of a triangle D to the end of the trapezoid as shown, to make the gable end of the house. Press toward triangle D.

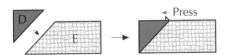

3. Trim rectangle G to make a trapezoid. Stitch the remaining triangle D to the end of the trapezoid, to make a rectangle. Press toward triangle D.

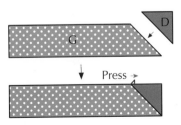

4. Draw a diagonal line on the wrong side of the rectangle made in step 3 by aligning the diagonal line on your Bias Square with the bottom edge of the rectangle, and the edge of the Bias Square with the upper right corner of the rectangle.

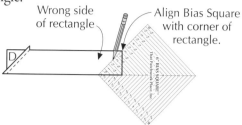

5. With right sides facing, place the rectangle made in step 4 together with the gable end of the roof (made in step 2). Sew the pieces together on the drawn diagonal line to complete the roof unit, which should measure 2½" x 12½". Refer to "Cut Corners" on page 55. Trim away the excess fabric. Press toward triangle E.

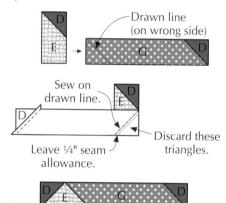

6. Sew sky/chimney unit to the roof unit. Press toward the sky unit. The resulting rectangle should measure 4½" x 12½".

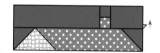

7. Stitch rectangles H and J together. Press toward rectangle H. Stitch a rectangle K to opposite sides as shown, to complete the door wall, which should measure 4½" x 6½". Press toward rectangle K.

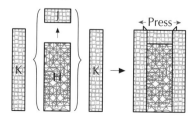

8. Sew rectangles I and L together to make the window strip. Press toward rectangle L. Stitch rectangles M and N in place to complete the window wall, 6½" x 12½". Press toward rectangles M and N.

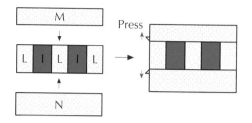

9. Stitch the window wall to the door wall. Press toward the door wall. The resulting rectangle should measure 6½" x 12½".

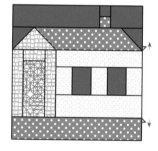

10. Sew the door/window wall unit to the sky/roof unit. Press toward the roof. Sew rectangle O in place, to add the grass. Press toward rectangle O.

11. To assemble your quilt, refer to "Settings," beginning on page 70.

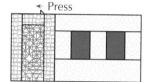

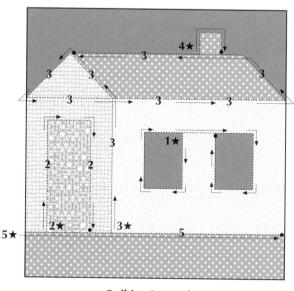

Quilting Suggestion
Arrows and numbers indicate stitching direction and order. See page 80.

Saltbox House

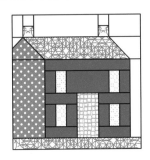
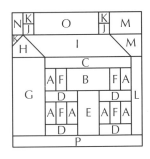

Cutting

- From the wall fabric for A and B, cut 1 strip, 2½" x 15"; crosscut into:
  - 6 rectangles, each 2½" x 1½", for A
  - 1 rectangle, 2½" x 4½", for B
- From the wall fabric for C and D, cut 1 strip, 1½" x 24"; crosscut into:
  - 1 rectangle, 1½" x 8½", for C
  - 4 rectangles, each 1½" x 3½", for D
- From the fabric for E, cut 1 rectangle, 2½" x 4½", for the door.
- From the fabric for F, cut 4 rectangles, each 1½" x 2½", for the windows.
- From the fabric for G, cut 1 rectangle, 3½" x 7½", for the side wall.
- From the fabric for H, cut 1 rectangle, 2½" x 3½", for the side wall.
- From the fabric for I, cut 1 rectangle, 2½" x 10½", for the roof.
- From the fabric for J, cut 2 squares, each 1½" x 1½", for the chimneys.
- From the sky fabric for K and L, cut 1 strip, 1½" x 13"; crosscut into:
  - 3 squares, each 1½" x 1½", for K
  - 1 rectangle, 1½" x 7½", for L
- From the sky fabric for M, N, and O, cut 1 strip, 2½" x 16"; crosscut into:
  - 2 rectangles, each 2½" x 3½", for M
  - 1 rectangle, 1½" x 2½", for N
  - 1 rectangle, 2½" x 6½", for O
- From the fabric for P, cut 1 rectangle, 1½" x 12½", for the grass.

Piecing

1. Stitch 2 A rectangles to opposite sides of a rectangle F as shown. Press toward rectangle A. Stitch a rectangle D to the top and bottom of each unit as shown to complete 2 lower window units. Press toward rectangle D.

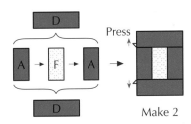

2. Stitch the units made in step 1 to each long side of rectangle E (door). Press toward rectangle E. The resulting unit should measure 4½" x 8½".

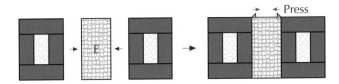

3. Stitch the remaining 2 A rectangles, 2 F rectangles, and rectangle B together as shown. Sew rectangle C to the resulting unit to make the upper-windows strip. Press toward rectangle C. The resulting unit should measure 3½" x 8½".

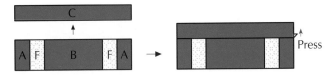

4. Sew the upper-windows strip to the lower-windows/door rectangle. Press toward the lower unit. The unit should now measure 7½" x 8½".

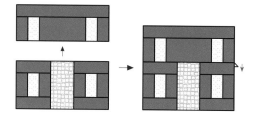

5. Stitch rectangles G and L to the sides of the unit made in step 4. Press toward rectangles G and L. Sew rectangle P to the bottom as shown. Press toward rectangle P. The house unit should now measure 8½" x 12½".

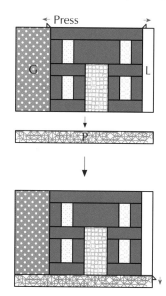

6. Stitch squares J and K together. Make 2 J/K units. Press toward square J. Sew the units together with rectangles M, N, and O, to make the sky/chimney unit. Press away from chimneys.

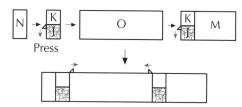

7. Draw a diagonal line on the wrong side of the remaining square K. Stitch to rectangle H to make a cut corner. Refer to "Cut Corners" on page 55. Press toward the triangle.

8. Draw 2 diagonal lines on the wrong side of rectangle I. Align the diagonal line on your Bias Square with the bottom edge of the rectangle as shown.

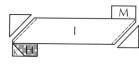

9. To complete the roof unit, stitch the cut-corner square made in step 7 and rectangle M to rectangle I on the drawn diagonal lines. Trim away the excess fabric. Press toward piece I. The resulting rectangle should measure 2½" x 12½".

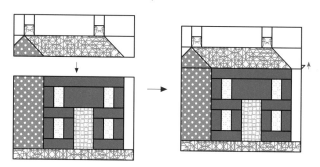

10. Sew the chimney strip to the roof and press toward the chimneys.

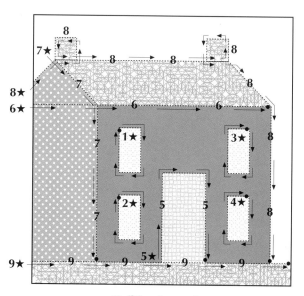

11. To assemble your quilt, refer to "Settings," beginning on page 70.

Quilting Suggestion
Arrows and numbers indicate stitching direction and order. See page 80.

Hanging Basket

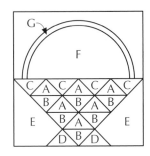

Cutting

- From the fabric for A, cut 1 rectangle, 3" x 9".
- From the fabric for B, cut 1 rectangle, 3" x 9".
- From the fabric for C, cut 2 squares, each 3" x 3". Cut each square once diagonally to yield 4 triangles.
- From the fabric for D, cut 1 square, 3⅞" x 3⅞".
- From the fabric for E, cut 1 square, 6⅞" x 6⅞". Cut the square once diagonally to yield 2 triangles.
- From the fabric for F, cut 1 rectangle, 6½" x 12½".
- From the fabric for G, cut 1 bias strip, 1" x 14". Refer to "Cutting a Bias Strip" below.

Piecing

1. Draw a grid with 3 squares, each 3" x 3", on the wrong side of rectangle B. Draw diagonal lines on each square. Refer to "Half-Square Triangle Units" on page 26.

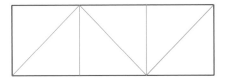

Cutting a Bias Strip

Make a bias cut in the fabric by aligning the 45° marking on your 6" x 24" cutting ruler

with a straight-of-grain edge of your fabric. Move the ruler along the fabric until you have a measurement of 14". Cut the fabric. Measure a 1"-wide strip, then cut to yield 1 bias strip, 1" x 14".

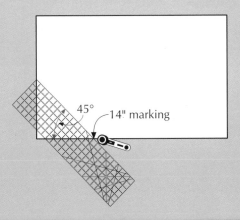

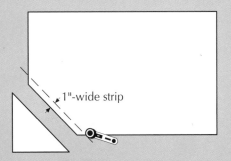

2. With right sides together, stitch rectangles A and B together. Cut apart to make 6 half-square triangle units, each 2⅝" x 2⅝". Press toward triangle B.

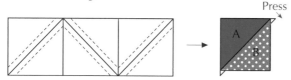

Press

A
B

3. Make 2 strips by sewing half-square triangle units and C triangles together as shown. Press.

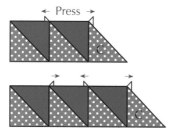

← Press →

C

C

4. Stitch the remaining half-square triangle unit and the remaining C triangles together to make a pieced triangle. The short sides of the resulting triangle should measure 5⅛". Press toward triangle C.
(*Hint:* Match the corners of the triangles with the corner of the square. The tips of the triangles will extend beyond the edges of the square.)

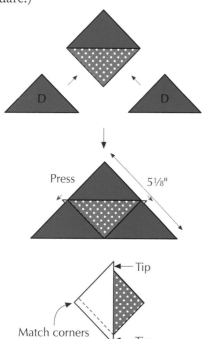

D
D

Press
5⅛"

Tip
Match corners
Tip

5. Sew the triangle made in step 4 to the strips made in step 3 to complete the basket center. The short sides should measure 9⅜". Press toward the triangle.

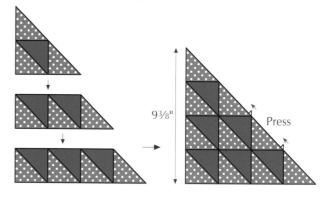

9⅜"
Press

6. Draw a diagonal line on the wrong side of square D. Cut the square in half on the diagonal, opposite the drawn line, to make 2 triangles.

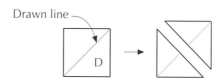

Drawn line

D

7. Align a triangle D with the corners of a triangle E as shown. Stitch triangles D and E together on the drawn diagonal line. Refer to "Cut Corners" on page 55. Trim away excess fabric. Make another unit that is a mirror image of the first. Press toward triangle E.

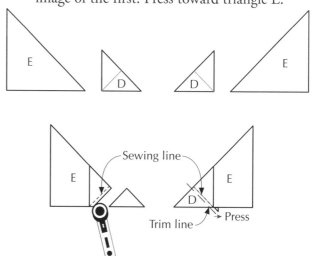

E
D
D
E

Sewing line

E
D
E

Trim line
Press

8. Stitch the triangles made in step 7 to the basket center. The resulting basket base should measure 6½" x 12½". Refer to "Flying Geese Units" on page 37. Press.

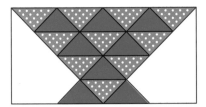

9. Fold rectangle F in half and finger-press a crease in the center. On the right side, use a compass to lightly draw an arc with a radius of 4¾". Be sure to place the point of the compass on the crease, ¼" inside the bottom edge of the fabric.

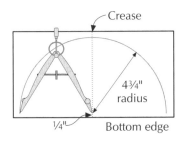

Crease

4¾" radius

¼" Bottom edge

10. Turn under ¼" and press one lengthwise edge of bias strip G. With right sides together, pin 1 end of the bias strip to the bottom edge of rectangle F. Gently curve the raw edge of the bias to match the curve of the drawn arc. Pin in place as you work. Your length of bias is generous, so do not stretch the bias too tightly or the rectangle will pucker. Sew the handle in place, ¼" from the raw edge of the bias strip.

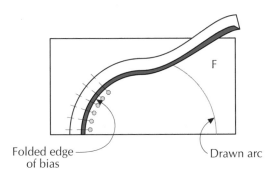

F

Folded edge of bias

Drawn arc

11. Flip the bias strip and pin in place so that the right side of the bias strip faces up. The folded edge becomes the top edge of the handle. Pin in place and, using a thread that matches the bias strip, machine stitch ⅛" inside the folded edge to complete the basket-handle unit, or blindstitch the edge by hand or machine instead.

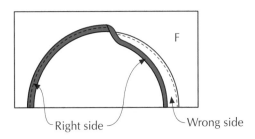

F

Right side Wrong side

12. Sew the basket-handle unit to the basket-base unit. Press toward the handle.

13. To assemble your quilt, refer to "Settings," beginning on page 70.

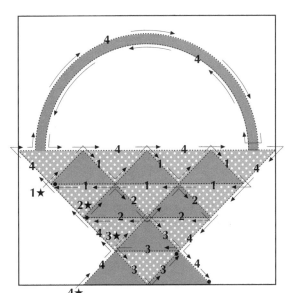

Quilting Suggestion
Arrows and numbers indicate stitching direction and order. See page 80.

Whirling Star

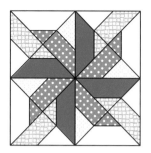
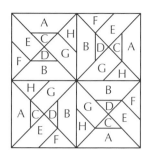

Cutting

- From the fabric for A, cut 1 square, 7¼" x 7¼".
  Cut the square twice diagonally to yield 4 triangles.
- From the fabric for B, cut 1 square, 7¼" x 7¼".
  Cut the square twice diagonally to yield 4 triangles.
- From the fabric for C, cut 4 squares, each 2¼" x 2¼".
- From the fabric for D, cut 4 squares, each 2¼" x 2¼".
- From the fabric for E, cut 4 rectangles, each 2¼" x 5⅛".
- From the fabric for F, cut 1 square, 4¾" x 4¾".
  Cut the square twice diagonally to yield 4 triangles.
- From the fabric for G, cut 4 rectangles, each 2¼" x 5⅛".
- From the fabric for H, cut 1 square, 4¾" x 4¾".
  Cut the square twice diagonally to yield 4 triangles.

Piecing

1. Draw a diagonal line on the wrong side of squares C and D. With right sides together, stitch triangle A and square C together, referring to "Cut Corners" on page 55. Stitch triangle B and square D together in the same manner. Trim away the excess fabric, leaving ¼"-wide seam allowances. The short sides of the resulting cut-corner triangles should measure 6⅞". Press toward triangles C and D.

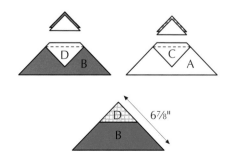

2. Trim one end of each rectangle E and G at a 45° angle to make 8 trapezoids. Refer to "Trapezoids" on page 34.

3. Arrange a trapezoid E with a triangle F, and a trapezoid G with a triangle H. Sew together to make 8 triangles that measure 6⅞" on the short sides. Press toward triangles F and H. (*Hint:* Match the corner of the triangle with the corner of the trapezoid as shown. The tips of the triangle will extend beyond the edges of the trapezoid.)

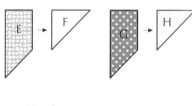
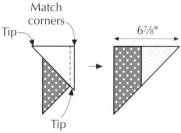

4. Sew the triangles made in step 3 and the triangles made in step 1 together along the short sides. Press.

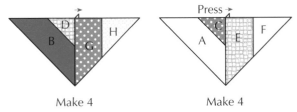

Make 4   Make 4

5. Arrange the 8 triangles made in step 4 as shown. Stitch together to make 4 squares, each 6½" x 6½". Press 2 squares in 1 direction and the other 2 squares in the opposite direction.

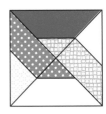

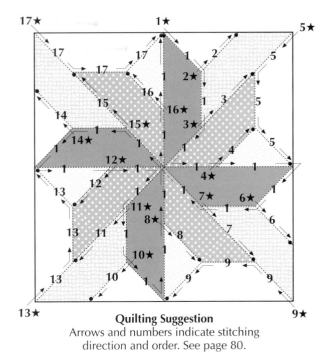

Quilting Suggestion
Arrows and numbers indicate stitching
direction and order. See page 80.

6. Match up the squares so each pair has seams pressed in opposite directions. Sew the squares together into 2 rows of 2 blocks each. Sew the rows together. Press in a counterclockwise direction, referring to "Pinwheel Centers" on page 41.

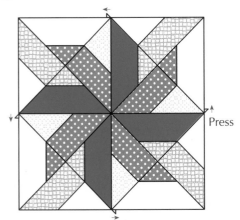

Press

7. To assemble your quilt, refer to "Settings," beginning on page 70.

Rocking Horse

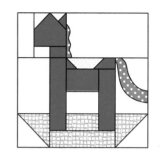
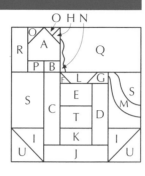

Cutting

- For the horse's body, cut:
    - 1 square, 3½" x 3½", for A
    - 1 strip, 2" x 16"; crosscut into:
        - 1 rectangle, 1½" x 2", for B
        - 1 rectangle, 2" x 7", for C
        - 1 rectangle, 2" x 6", for D
    - 1 rectangle, 2½" x 3½", for E
    - 1 square, 1½" x 1½", for F
    - 1 rectangle, 1½" x 2½", for G
    - 1 square, 2" x 2", for H
- For the rocker, cut:
    - 1 square, 3⅞" x 3⅞", for I
    - 1 rectangle, 2" x 6½", for J
    - 1 rectangle, 2" x 3½", for K
- For the saddle, cut:
    - 1 rectangle, 1½" x 4", for L
- For the mane and tail, cut:
    - 1 rectangle, 3½" x 4½", for M
    - 1 rectangle, 1" x 4", for N
- For the background, cut:
    - 2 squares, each 2" x 2", for O
    - 1 rectangle, 1½" x 2", for P
    - 1 rectangle, 4½" x 8", for Q
    - 1 rectangle, 2" x 4½", for R
    - 2 rectangles, each 3½" x 5½", for S
    - 1 rectangle, 2½" x 3½", for T
    - 1 square, 3⅞" x 3⅞", for U

Piecing

Templates for horse's mane and tail are on page 69.

1. Draw a diagonal line on the wrong side of 1 square O. With right sides together, stitch squares O and H together on the diagonal line to make a 2" x 2" cut-corner square. Refer to "Cut Corners" on page 55. Trim away excess fabric. Press toward triangle H.

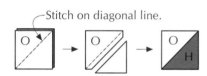

2. Draw a diagonal line on the wrong side of the cut-corner square, opposite the just-sewn seam. With right sides together, stitch the cut-corner square to square A on the diagonal line. The resulting square measures 3½" x 3½". Press seam toward H/O unit.

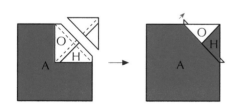

3. Draw a diagonal line on the wrong side of the remaining square O. Place it on the corner adjacent to the just-completed corner. Stitch in place to make another cut corner. Press toward triangle O.

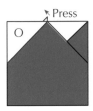

4. Stitch rectangle B to rectangle P along the short sides. Press toward rectangle P. Sew the unit to the bottom of the unit made in step 3, the horse's head. Press toward the head.

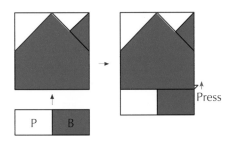

5. Stitch rectangle R to the left side of the horse's head. Press toward the rectangle.

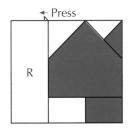

6. Using the mane template, trace the design onto the right side of rectangle N. With right sides facing up, align the mane in the corner of rectangle Q as shown. Appliqué the wavy edge of the mane to the rectangle with a machine satin stitch. If you choose to blindstitch by hand or machine, add a 3⁄16" seam allowance to the wavy edge.

Appliquéd edge

7. Sew rectangle Q to the right side of the horse's head. Press toward the mane. The unit should measure 4½" x 12½".

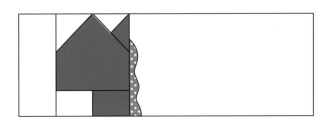

8. Draw 2 diagonal lines on the wrong side of rectangle L as shown. Align the diagonal line on your Bias Square with the bottom edge of the rectangle. Stitch square F and rectangle G in place to make the saddle unit. Refer to "Cut Corners" on page 55. Press toward piece L.

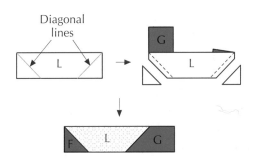

Diagonal lines

9. Sew rectangles E, T, and K together as shown. Press away from rectangle T. Stitch rectangle D in place. Press toward rectangle D.

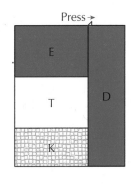

10. Sew the saddle unit to the top of the unit made in step 9. Press toward the saddle. Sew rectangle C in place. Press toward rectangle C.

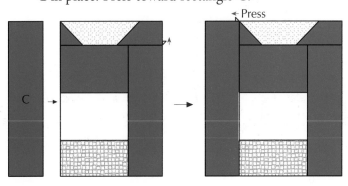

11. Stitch rectangle J in place to complete the horse-body unit. Press toward rectangle J.

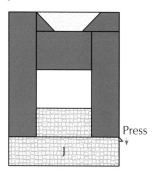

12. Draw a diagonal line on the wrong side of square U. With right sides together, stitch squares U and I together to make 2 half-square triangle units, each 3½" x 3½". Refer to "Half-Square Triangle Units" on page 26.

Make 2

13. Using the tail template, trace the design onto the right side of rectangle M. With right sides facing up, align the tail in the corner of 1 rectangle S as shown. Appliqué the curved edges to the rectangle, using a machine satin stitch. If you choose to blindstitch by hand or machine, add a ³⁄₁₆" seam allowance to the curved edges.

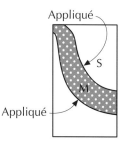

Appliqué

Appliqué

14. Stitch a half-square triangle unit to the tail unit and to the remaining rectangle S. Press toward the rectangles.

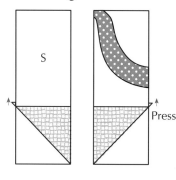

15. Sew horse-body unit and the units completed in step 14 together as shown. Press away from rectangle S.

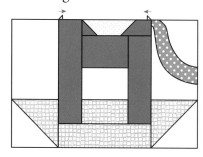

16. Stitch the units completed in steps 7 and 15 together as shown. Press toward the horse's head.

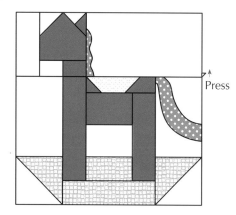

17. To assemble your quilt, refer to "Settings," beginning on page 70.

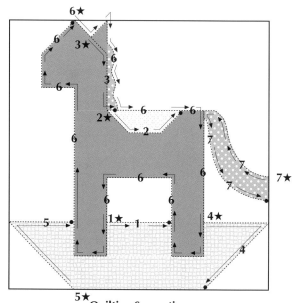

Quilting Suggestion
Arrows and numbers indicate stitching direction and order. See page 80.

Rocking Horse Block
Appliqué Templates

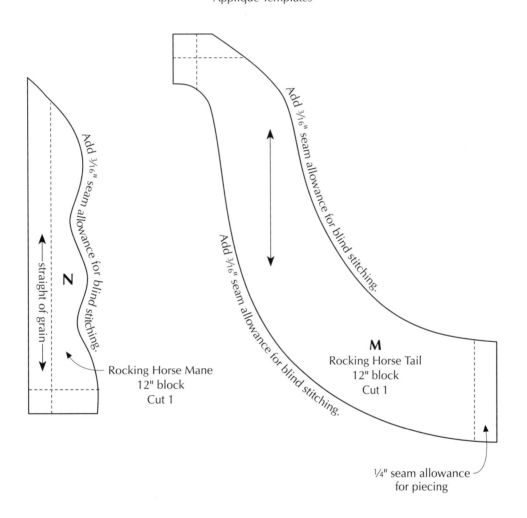

Add ³⁄₁₆" seam allowance for blind stitching.

← straight of grain →

N

Rocking Horse Mane
12" block
Cut 1

Add ³⁄₁₆" seam allowance for blind stitching.

Add ³⁄₁₆" seam allowance for blind stitching.

M
Rocking Horse Tail
12" block
Cut 1

¼" seam allowance
for piecing

Settings

The term "setting" is used to describe how quilt blocks are arranged. In all the quilts in this book, the blocks are set side by side and separated by corners and sashings. The corners and sashings can highlight or disguise the quilt setting.

If you want to highlight the setting, choose fabrics that are different than the background fabric, but don't overpower the main fabric. Accent fabrics work well. For examples, look at "Stars in My Corner" (page 14), "Northern Houses" (page 16), and "Beginner's Sampler" (page 20).

If you want to disguise the setting, choose fabrics that blend with (or use) the background fabric. For examples, look at "Whirling Stars" (page 15) and "Ships That Pass in the Night" (page 17).

Rules are made to be broken; look at "Samurai Dance" (page 13) and "Painted Ponies" (page 15). The sashings in "Samurai Dance" are actually made from the main fabric in this quilt. This Japanese-print fabric ties the different accent and background fabrics together. In "Painted Ponies," the medium- and dark-value fabrics used for the pinwheel corners and double sashing produce a three-dimensional, Attic Windows effect.

Corners and Sashings

This section includes yardage and cutting charts, assembly instructions, and illustrations for the corners and sashings. All measurements include ¼"-wide seam allowances.

I've included three corner and five sashing designs that you can mix and match. Choose a combination used in one of the quilts in the gallery on pages 13–20 or develop your own combination to suit your blocks. As long as the corners are 3½" square and the sashing strips are 3½" x 12½", you won't alter the quilt size or the instructions for adding borders and finishing.

 # Plain Corners

Plain Corners Yardage Chart
Materials: 44"-wide fabric • Fabric Requirements in Yards

Runner/Wall	Crib	Lap	Twin	Full/Queen	King
⅛	¼	¼	⅜	⅜	½

Plain Corners Cutting Chart
Cut all strips across the width of the fabric (crosswise grain).

		Runner	Wall	Crib	Lap	Twin	Full/Queen	King
1st Cut ➤	3½"-wide strips	1	1	2	2	3	3	4
2nd Cut ➤	3½" squares							
	Finished Corners	10	9	12	20	24	30	36

 **Four-Patch Corners**

Four-Patch Corners Yardage Chart

Materials: 44"-wide fabric • *Fabric Requirements in Yards*

	Runner/Wall	Crib	Lap	Twin	Full/Queen	King
Fabric A	⅛	¼	¼	¼	¼	⅜
Fabric B	⅛	¼	¼	¼	¼	⅜

Four-Patch Corners Cutting Chart

Cut all strips across the width of the fabric (crosswise grain).

	Runner	Wall	Crib	Lap	Twin	Full/Queen	King
1st Cut ➤ 2"-wide strips							
Fabric A	1	1	2	2	3 ✓	3	4
Fabric B	1	1	2	2	3 ✓	3	4

Sew the strips together along the long side. Press toward the darker fabric.

	Runner	Wall	Crib	Lap	Twin	Full/Queen	King
2nd Cut ➤ 2" x 3½" segments							
Segment A/B	20	18	24	40	48 ✓	60	72

Referring to the illustration below, sew the segments together to complete the Four-Patch corners. Press in either direction.

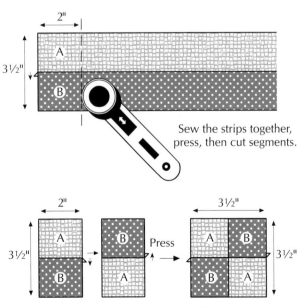

Sew the strips together, press, then cut segments.

Press

Sew the segments together.

Nine-Patch Corners

Nine-Patch Corners Yardage Chart

Materials: 44"-wide fabric   •   Fabric Requirements in Yards

	Runner/Wall	Crib	Lap	Twin	Full/Queen	King
Fabric A	¼	¼	¼	¼	⅜	⅜
Fabric B	¼	¼	¼	¼	⅜	⅜

Nine-Patch Corners Cutting Chart

Cut all strips across the width of the fabric (crosswise grain).

	Runner	Wall	Crib	Lap	Twin	Full/Queen	King
1st Cut ➤ 1½"-wide strips							
Fabric A	3	3	3	4	4	7	7
Fabric B	3	3	3	5	5	8	8

Sew a strip A to each side of strip B. Press toward strip B. Sew a strip B to each side of the remaining A strips. Press toward B strips.

Strip Sets	Runner	Wall	Crib	Lap	Twin	Full/Queen	King
A/B/A	1	1	1	1	1	3	3
B/A/B	1	1	1	2	2	2	2
2nd Cut ➤ 1½" x 3½" segments							
A/B/A	10	9	12	20	24	30	36
B/A/B	20	18	24	40	48	60	72

Referring to the illustration below, sew the segments together to complete the Nine-Patch corners. Press toward the B/A/B sets.

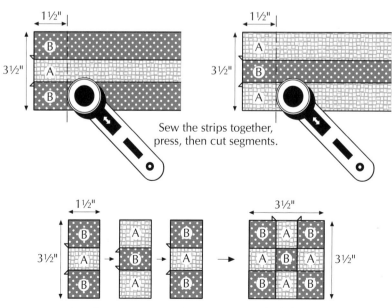

Sew the strips together, press, then cut segments.

Sew the segments together. Press toward B/A/B sets.

Pinwheel Corners

Pinwheel Corners Yardage Chart

Materials: 44"-wide fabric • Fabric Requirements in Yards

	Runner/Wall	Crib	Lap	Twin	Full/Queen	King
Fabric A	¼	¼	¼	¼	⅜	⅜
Fabric B	¼	¼	¼	¼	⅜	⅜

Pinwheel Corners Cutting Chart

Cut all strips across the width of the fabric (crosswise grain).

	Runner	Wall	Crib	Lap	Twin	Full/Queen	King
1st Cut ➤ 2⅜"-wide strips							
Fabric A	2	2	2	3	3	4	5
Fabric B	2	2	2	3	3	4	5
2nd Cut ➤ 2⅜" x 4¾" rectangles							
Fabric A	10	9	12	20	24	30	36
Fabric B	10	9	12	20	24	30	36

Using your C-Thru ruler, draw lines every 2⅜" on the wrong side of each rectangle A. Draw a diagonal line on each square. With right sides together, place each rectangle B on a rectangle A. Align the raw edges. Using ¼"-wide seam allowances, stitch along both sides of the diagonal lines.

Cut on the drawn lines. Open and press toward fabric B. You should have 4 finished 2" half-square triangle units for each rectangle.

Sew 4 half-square triangle units together to make each Pinwheel corner. See "Pinwheel Centers" on page 41 for pressing instructions.

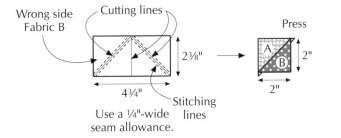

Wrong side Fabric B — Cutting lines — 2⅜" — 4¾" — Use a ¼"-wide seam allowance. — Stitching lines — Press — 2" — 2"

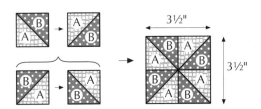

Sew the 4 half-square triangle units together.

Tip

If you want a three-dimensional effect (as in "Painted Ponies," page 15), use medium- and dark-value fabrics. Arrange the finished corners and sashings to spin opposite each other before you sew.

 # Mini-star Corners

Mini-star Corners Yardage Chart

Materials: 44"-wide fabric • Fabric Requirements in Yards

	Runner/Wall	Crib	Lap	Twin	Full/Queen	King
Fabric A	1/8	1/8	1/4	1/4	1/4	1/4
Fabric B	1/8	1/8	1/4	1/4	1/4	3/8
Fabric C	1/8	1/8	1/8	1/8	1/4	1/4
Fabric D	1/8	1/8	1/8	1/8	1/8	1/8

Mini-star Corners Cutting Chart

Cut all strips across the width of the fabric (crosswise grain).

	Runner	Wall	Crib	Lap	Twin	Full/Queen	King
1st Cut ▶ Fabric A (2¾"-wide strips)	1	1	1	2	2	2	3
Fabric B (1⅝"-wide strips)	2	2	2	4	4	5	6
Fabric C (1¼"-wide strips)	2	1	2	3	3	4	5
Fabric D (2"-wide strips)	1	1	1	1	2	2	2
2nd Cut ▶ Fabric A (2¾" squares)	10	9	12	20	24	30	36
Fabric B (1⅝" squares)	40	36	48	80	96	120	144
Fabric C (1¼" squares)	40	36	48	80	96	120	144
Fabric D (2" squares)	10	9	12	20	24	30	36

3rd Cut ▶ Cut the 2¾" fabric A squares twice on the diagonal to yield 4 triangles from each fabric A square.

Cut the 1⅝" fabric B squares once on the diagonal to yield 2 triangles from each fabric B square.

Refer to "Flying Geese Units" on page 37. Sew triangles A and B together to make 4 Flying Geese units (for each Mini-star corner). Press toward B triangles.

Sew a square C to each side of 2 Flying Geese units to make 2 Flying Geese strips. Press toward square C.

Sew 2 Flying Geese units to opposite sides of square D. Press toward square D.

Sew the rows together. Press toward square D.

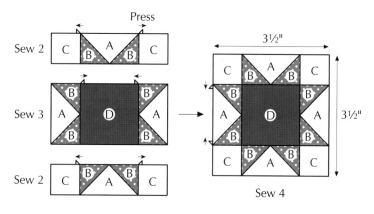

Tip

Because there are so many seams in these small stars, the edges tend to roll up. To keep them flat, spray them with water as you press. Attaching the mini-stars to the quilt will solve the problem.

Plain Sashings

Plain Sashings Yardage Chart

Materials: 44"-wide fabric • Fabric Requirements in Yards

Runner	Wall	Crib	Lap	Twin	Full/Queen	King
⅝	½	⅝	1¼	1½	1¾	2¼

Plain Sashings Cutting Chart

Cut all strips across the width of the fabric (crosswise grain).

	Runner	Wall	Crib	Lap	Twin	Full/Queen	King
1st Cut ➤ 3½"-wide strips	5	4	6	11	13	17	20
2nd Cut ➤ 3½" x 12½" rectangles	13	12	17	31	38	49	60

Double Sashings

Double Sashings Yardage Chart

Materials: 44"-wide fabric • Fabric Requirements in Yards

	Runner	Wall	Crib	Lap	Twin	Full/Queen	King
Fabric A	⅜	⅜	½	¾	⅞	1	1¼
Fabric B	⅜	⅜	½	¾	⅞	1	1¼

Double Sashings Cutting Chart

Cut all strips across the width of the fabric (crosswise grain).

	Runner	Wall	Crib	Lap	Twin	Full/Queen	King
1st Cut ➤ 2"-wide strips							
Fabric A	5	4	6	11	13	17	20
Fabric B	5	4	6	11	13	17	20
2nd Cut ➤ Sew strips A and B together as shown. Press toward strip B.							
3½" x 12½" rectangles	13	12	17	31	38	49	60

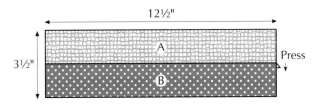

 # Triple Sashings

Triple Sashings Yardage Chart

Materials: 44"-wide fabric • Fabric Requirements in Yards

	Runner/Wall	Crib	Lap	Twin	Full/Queen	King
Fabric A	¼	⅜	½	⅝	¾	1
Fabric B	½	⅝	1	1¼	1½	1¾

Triple Sashings Cutting Chart

Cut all strips across the width of the fabric (crosswise grain).

	Runner	Wall	Crib	Lap	Twin	Full/Queen	King
1st Cut ➤ 1½"-wide strips							
Fabric A	5	4	6	11	13	17	20
Fabric B	9	8	12	21	26	33	40
Sew a strip B to each side of a strip A. Press toward strip B.							
2nd Cut ➤ 3½" x 12½" rectangles	13	12	17	31	38	49	60

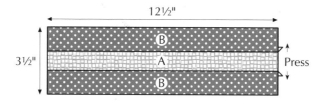

Adding Corners and Sashings to the Blocks

Refer to the "Quilt Assembly Plan" below as you arrange and assemble the completed blocks, corners, and sashings. This plan shows the location of each block for all the quilt sizes.

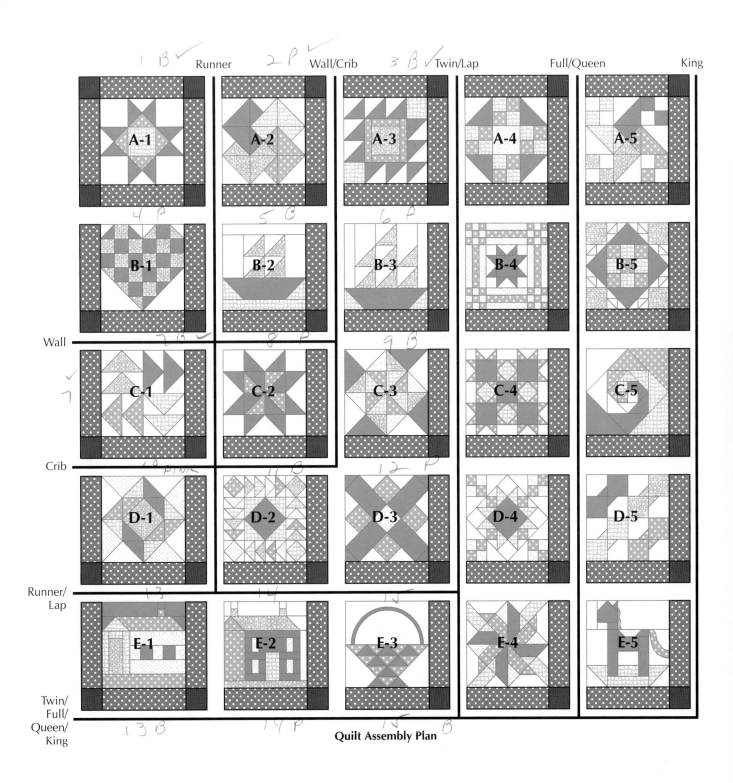

Quilt Assembly Plan

1. Sew a sashing strip to the bottom of each block. Press toward the sashing.
2. Sew a corner to the short side of each remaining sashing. Press toward the sashing. You should have one corner left; set it aside for now.
3. Sew a sashing unit to the right side of every block. Press toward the sashing unit.

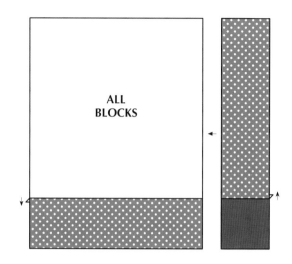

4. Arrange your blocks, then number them as shown in the "Quilt Assembly Plan" on page 77. This will help you stay organized as you assemble the quilt. Pin a numbered scrap of paper on the top of each block.

   Lay the remaining sashing units on the left side of the blocks in the first vertical column and along the top of the first horizontal row.

5. Sew a sashing unit to the left side of the blocks in the first vertical column (A-1, B-1, C-1, D-1, and/or E-1). Press toward the sashing unit.

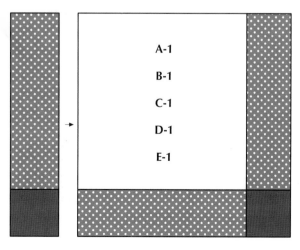

6. Sew a sashing unit to the top of the blocks in the first horizontal column (A-2, A-3, A-4, and/or A-5). Press toward the sashing unit.

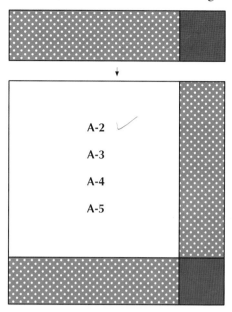

7. Sew the corner that you set aside in step 2 to one of the sashing units and press. Sew this sashing unit to the top of block A-1. Press toward the sashing unit.

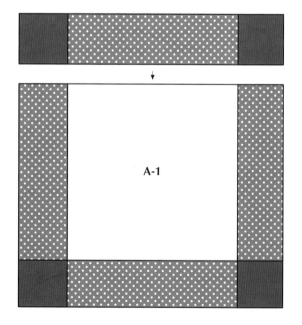

Backing, Batting, and Layering

Refer to the "Quilt Assembly Plan" on page 77. With the exception of block A-1, each backing section can be cut from a fat quarter. You will need ⅔ yard backing fabric for block A-1.

Use fabrics from your stash to piece a patchwork backing or use one fabric. A busy fabric helps disguise the seams in the backing.

The backing and batting are cut larger than the finished sizes to allow for shifting and shrinkage during the quilting process.

Block Backing Yardage Chart

Materials: 44"-wide fabric • Fabric Requirements in Yards

Runner	Wall	Crib	Lap	Twin	Full	Queen	King
1¼	1¼	1¾	3¼	4¼	5¼	5¼	6¾

1. Referring to the Block Backing and Batting Cutting Chart below, cut your backings and battings for each block.
2. Lay a backing piece right side down and place the batting on top, matching the edges. Center a block, right side up, on the batting. As you layer, smooth each piece from the center out. *Make sure that you are using the correct-size backing and batting with each block.* The 18" squares will be too small for a block in the first horizontal or vertical row.

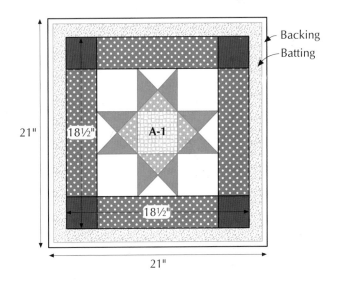

Block Backing and Batting Cutting Chart

	Runner	Wall	Crib	Lap	Twin	Full/Queen	King
Block A-1							
21" x 21"	1	1	1	1	1	1	1
First Vertical Row (Blocks B-1, C-1, D-1, E-1)							
18" x 21"	3	1	2	3	4	4	4
All Other Blocks							
18" x 18"		1	2	6	8	12	16
First Horizontal Row (Blocks A-2, A-3, A-4, A-5)							
18" x 21"		1	1	2	2	3	4

Basting

The feed dogs cause the backing to feed at a slightly faster rate than the top. When you add batting, the difference is even more pronounced. A walking foot and extra pins help.

Using flower-head straight pins, pin-baste. Place pins about 1" apart. Pin one line of quilting and stitch, removing the pins as you go. After each line of quilting, re-smooth your block. Repeat this procedure for all the quilt lines in the block.

Start and end your pinning beyond your stitching lines. This helps keep your backing flat as it enters the machine and prevents tucks from forming on the backing. To prevent tucks where quilting lines intersect, pin from the intersection out or from the center of the block out.

After pin-basting, check the backing. Repin if your backing is not smooth.

Machine Quilting

In-the-Ditch Quilting

The primary purpose of quilting is to hold the layers of the quilt together. Sampler quilts derive most of their visual interest from the piecing and settings and don't require fancy quilting. I've provided in-the-ditch quilting instructions with the directions for each block. They were planned to emphasize the block designs and add depth. When you press seams to one side, the side with the seam allowance forms a slight ridge. The side without the seam allowances is the "ditch." The side of the needle should almost touch the ridge as you stitch. When you stitch in-the-ditch, your machine quilting lines disappear.

At the end of the piecing instructions for each block is a machine-quilting suggestion. Quilt each block in-the-ditch, *following the lines in numerical order.* The start of each numbered stitching line is marked with a star, and the end with a dot. Pivot at a bend in

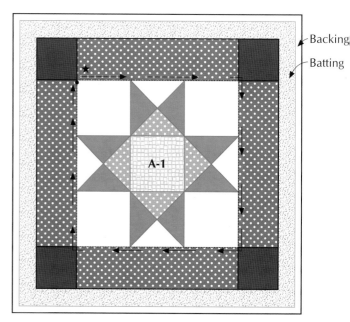

a line. It helps to follow the lines with your finger or trace the arrows using different-colored pencils before you quilt.

Since you will be quilting block by block, pivoting and gentle curves are not a problem. You can keep your feed dogs up as you quilt the blocks, sashings, corners, and borders.

Tip

If you have never machine quilted before, read through the instructions and practice before you start on your blocks. Sandwich an 8" square of batting between two 8" squares of fabric and try the techniques described in this section. You may want to use a pieced block for the top layer so you can practice stitching in-the-ditch.

Machine quilting produces twice as many threads as hand quilting; you have to tie off both the top and bottom at the beginning and end of each line of quilting. Therefore, you'll want to keep starting and stopping to a minimum. Try the following techniques to start and stop stitching.

1. Set your stitch length to 0 or use a very short stitch. Take three or four stitches at the beginning of your quilting line, then increase your stitch length to about ten stitches per inch and continue quilting the line. Reduce your stitch length to 0 or use very short stitches to end the quilting line; cut the threads.
2. Backstitch three or four stitches at the beginning and end of a quilt line and cut the threads.
3. Stitch the line. Lift the backing fabric and pull the loose threads to the middle layer of the quilt and tie them off. This method is my personal favorite. I tie the threads of each quilting line as I go. The machine-quilting diagrams are designed around this method.
4. If you find any loose threads after machine quilting, thread them on a hand-sewing needle and bury them in the batting as you would if you were hand quilting.

After you have quilted the blocks, stitch in-the-ditch between the block, sashings, and corners. (Refer to the "Quilt Assembly Plan" on page 77.) *Do not quilt the sashings or corners until after they are attached to another block or row.*

Troubleshooting

If you are having trouble with machine quilting, try some of the following tips. Consult your sewing-machine manual before making any adjustments.

1. If you are having trouble staying in-the-ditch, pull the quilt taut on each side of the presser foot as you sew. This will help you see the ditch.
2. Adjust your stitch length.
3. Reduce the tension on your top thread.
4. If you have tucks in the backing, reduce the tension on your bobbin thread. If you have loose threads, increase the tension on your bobbin thread.
5. If your machine has an adjustment for the pressure on the presser foot, lessen the pressure.
6. Invest in a walking foot. This foot prevents tucks from forming in the quilt top and backing as you machine quilt. It is especially helpful if you are using polyester batting.

Additional Quilting

In-the-ditch quilting may not be enough for some blocks if you use cotton batting. Read the batting manufacturer's recommendations for information on the amount of quilting needed. Try these easy ways to add extra quilting.

- Use the C-Thru ruler and a chalk pencil (that shows up on your fabric) to echo the shapes in the block. For a large triangle like the one in the Prairie Queen block (page 29), add triangles to the center.

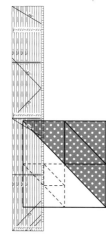

- To add continuous quilting lines, find the center point of each line in the particular shape and draw lines connecting those points. Repeat to add smaller and smaller shapes. As you stitch, detour to include these lines.

Center point of the line

- In some cases, you may want to add simple straight-line quilting. For boat bottoms and rooftops, I draw straight parallel lines in the trapezoid, stitch these lines, tie off the threads, then stitch, following the machine-quilting diagram.

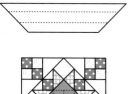

You may also want to add hand quilting. Hand quilting shows up well inside basket handles or large spaces like the centers of the Windblown Square (page 50) and Sailor's Star (page 54) blocks.

Assembling the Quilt

Once the blocks are quilted, you are ready to assemble the quilt! You will quilt the sashings and corners as you assemble the blocks into rows and the rows into the quilt.

Trimming the Blocks

Trim all four sides of each block before machine quilting the sashing or attaching it to another block. For the sides of the blocks that *have* sashing and corners, trim the batting and backing ½" beyond the edge of the sashing. For the sides of the blocks that *don't* have sashing and corners, trim the backing and batting even with the block edges.

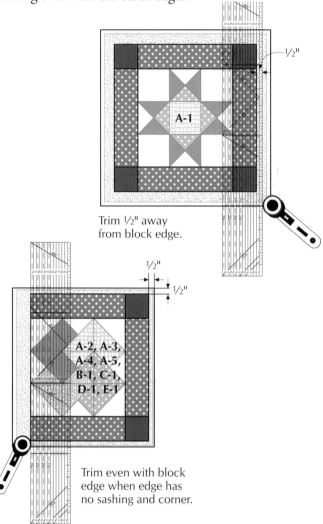

Trim ½" away from block edge.

Trim even with block edge when edge has no sashing and corner.

Sewing the Blocks Together

Machine quilt the vertical sashings as you sew the blocks together to make rows. Machine quilt the horizontal sashings and corners as you sew the rows together to form the quilt. I've designed a simple cable motif (page 95) that gives the illusion of continuous quilting. The curves are gentle and easy to sew. This motif will fit any of the sashings in the book, but feel free to try a pattern of your own. You can also stitch in-the-ditch of pieced corners and sashings.

Tip

Remember to center the template on the sashings based on their *finished* size; position the template ¼" closer to the edge of the quilt block if necessary.

1. Transfer the "Sashing Quilting Template" on page 95 to template plastic. Make sure to transfer the placement guides on the template. You can use the placement guides to help you line up and center the template on your sashings.

2. Start with the vertical sashing on the left side of block A-1. Place the template face down on your sashing and trace around it with your chalk pencil. Since you haven't attached the border, position the template ¼" closer to the edge of the block than to the outer edge of the sashing so it will be centered. Pin well and machine quilt.

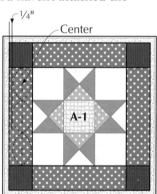

Tip

An unquilted sashing can be slightly larger than the quilted block or row to which it is being attached. Match up the edges and seams and pin often to ease in any extra sashing fabric. You won't notice the extra sashing fabric after the area has been quilted.

3. Pay careful attention to the orientation of the blocks in the illustrations. Turn block A-1 over to the back as shown. Fold back batting and backing of the unquilted vertical sashing and pin in place. Set aside.

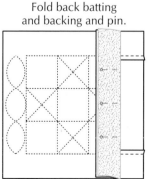

Fold back batting and backing and pin.

Back Side of Block A-1

4. Turn block A-2 over to the back. Fold back the batting and backing from the bottom sashing and pin in place as shown. Turn the block right side up. Make sure the vertical sashing is on the left-hand side of the block and the pinned sashing is on the top.

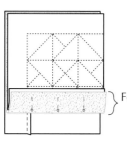

Fold back batting and backing and pin.

Back Side of Block A-2

5. Refer to the illustration below. Place block A-1, right side down, on top of block A-2. Pin the corner of block A-1 to the sashing of block A-2. Stitch the corner to the sashing, using a ¼"-wide seam allowance. Do not sew beyond the corner and do not catch the batting or backing. It must remain free so you can sew the rows of blocks together later. Remove the pins to release the batting and backing of block A-2.

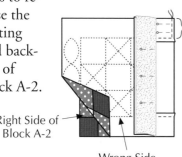

Right Side of Block A-2

Pin the block together, then stitch through top layers only.

Wrong Side of Block A-1

6. With block A-2 on the bottom, pin only the sashing of block A-1 to all the layers of block A-2. Begin stitching where you ended in step 5. Stitch through all the layers as shown, removing pins as you reach them. Remove the pins to release the batting and backing of block A-1.

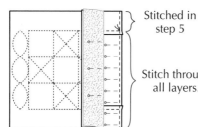

Stitched in step 5

Stitch through all layers.

7. With the backing side face up, lay the 2-block unit flat as shown. Trim the batting on block A-1 even with the edge of the sashing on block A-2.

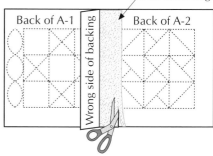

Trim batting even with seam edge.

Back of A-1   Wrong side of backing   Back of A-2

8. Fold over and turn under the backing of block A-1 (about ⅝") so the folded edge just covers the stitching that joins the blocks. Pin. Check to make sure that the sashing on the front side is lying smooth and flat. If it doesn't, remove the pins and repin. (You may have pulled the backing too tight.)

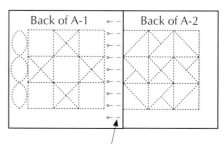

Back of A-1   Back of A-2

Fold backing over seam and pin.

9. Turn the unit over and pin in-the-ditch of the seam between the blocks and sashing. Pins should point toward the top edge of the blocks. Check the back side to make sure that the pins have caught the folded edge. If not, adjust the folded edge and repin from the front. Then, remove the pins on the back.

Working from the front side of the unit, machine quilt in-the-ditch through all layers, stitching from the top edge toward the bottom and removing the pins as you reach them. End the stitching at the top of the sashing as shown below.

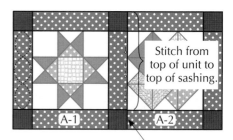

Stitch from top of unit to top of sashing.

A-1   A-2

Stitch this portion of the seam from the back side in step 10.

10. Turn the unit over. Machine or hand stitch only through the backing of the unstitched edge as shown below.

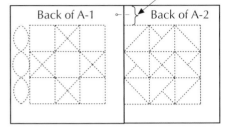

Stitch through the backing only.

11. Working from the front, machine quilt the sashing between blocks A-1 and A-2, as you did the sashing at the left of block A-1 in step 2.

12. Repeat steps 2–11 with the remaining blocks in row A. At the end of the row, quilt the sashing on the right-hand side of the last block.

13. Assemble all remaining rows except the last one in the same manner as you did row A. For the last row, stitch from the top edge to the bottom edge of each block, instead of stopping for the corner as you did in step 5.

Sewing the Rows Together

Refer to "The Quilt Assembly Plan" on page 77 and "Sewing the Blocks Together," beginning on page 83.

1. Mark the sashings and corners at the top of the blocks; remember to allow ¼" for the seam allowance when positioning the template. The quilting lines should meet in the center of each side of the corners. To mark the corners, connect the quilting lines as shown.

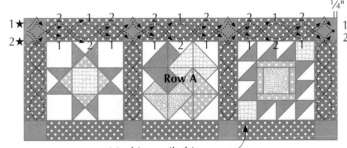

Machine quilt this row after you attach row B.

2. Pin-baste the first line of quilting and stitch. When you reach the end of the row, take the quilt out of the machine, tie and clip your threads, and begin sewing again from where you started. Do not pivot. If you pivot at the end of a long row of quilting, your quilt top or backing may shift.

3. Fold back the batting and the backing on the bottom of row A and pin as you did when joining the blocks. Lay row B on top of row A, right sides together. Match up the edges and seams and pin the row of sashings and corners of row A through all the layers of row B. Pin about every inch. Stitch the rows together.

4. Turn the rows over to the back side and lay them flat. Unpin the batting and backing from the back of row A. Fold over and trim the batting even with the edge of the stitching that joins the rows.

5. Working from the back side of the rows, turn under the backing on row A approximately ⅝" so that it just covers the seam line. Pin. Make sure that the sashing on the front side of the quilt lies flat. If it doesn't, repin.

6. Working from the front of the rows, pin in-the-ditch between the blocks and sashing. Check the back side to make sure that your pins catch the folded edge. Remove the pins from the back side. Machine quilt in-the-ditch across the entire row, removing the pins as you reach them.

7. Referring to steps 1 and 2, machine quilt the sashings and corners between rows A and B. Take the quilt out of the machine and tie off your threads.

8. Following the steps above, continue assembling and quilting the rows. You may want to machine quilt the last horizontal row of sashings and corners before attaching the row. Trim the batting and backing even with the edges. You are ready to add the borders (pages 86–88) or bind your quilt (pages 89–90).

Tip

As the quilt gets larger and harder to handle, keep the bulk of the quilt to your left as you sew so most of it is away from the arm of the machine.

Borders

There are some special considerations when making borders for your Block by Block quilt. Since it has already been quilted, it may have changed size. To allow for this change, the border measurements in the charts include approximately an extra 4" in length.

As long as your quilt measures within 3" of the size listed in the "Quilt Size Chart" (page 7), you can use the single and double border charts in this section. Otherwise, refer to "Customizing Your Quilt Borders" on page 88.

Cut your borders across the width (crosswise grain) of your fabric. You will need to piece most of the borders, backings, and batting. Refer to page 12 for batting yardage.

Single Border

Single Border Yardage Chart
Materials: 44"-wide fabric   •   Fabric Requirements in Yards

	Runner/Wall	Crib	Lap	Twin	Full	Queen	King
Single Border	1	1¼	1¾	2	2	3	3¼
Backing	1½	1½	2½	2¾	3	4	4¼

Single Border Cutting Chart
Cut and piece 2 of each for the following. Cut the backing and batting pieces 2" longer and 2" wider than the borders.

	Runner	Wall	Crib	Lap	Twin	Full	Queen	King
Sides	5" x 68"	6½" x 38"	6½" x 53"	8½" x 68"	8½" x 83"	8½" x 83"	11½" x 83"	11½" x 83"
Top and Bottom	5" x 32"	6½" x 50"	6½" x 50"	8½" x 69"	8½" x 69"	8½" x 84"	11½" x 90"	11½" x 105"

Refer to "Machine Quilting and Attaching the Borders" on page 88.

Double Border

Double Border Yardage Chart
Materials: 44"-wide fabric   •   Fabric Requirements in Yards

	Runner/Wall	Crib	Lap	Twin	Full	Queen	King
Inner Border	⅜	½	¾	¾	1	1¼	1¼
Outer Border	¾	1	1¼	1¼	1½	2	2¼
Backing	1½	1½	2½	2¾	3	4	4¼

Double Border Cutting Chart

Cut 2 of each for the following. Cut the backing and batting pieces so they are 2" longer and 2" wider than the finished, pieced borders.

	Runner	Wall	Crib	Lap	Twin	Full	Queen	King
Inner Sides	2" x 68"	2½" x 38"	2½" x 53"	3½" x 68"	3½" x 83"	3½" x 83"	4½" x 83"	4½" x 83"
Inner Top and Bottom	2" x 21½"	2½" x 37½"	2½" x 37½"	3½" x 54½"	3½" x 54½"	3½" x 69½"	4½" x 71½"	4½" x 86½"
Outer Sides	3½" x 68"	4½" x 38"	4½" x 53"	5½" x 68"	5½" x 83"	5½" x 83"	7½" x 83"	7½" x 83"
Outer Top and Bottom	3½" x 32"	4½" x 50"	4½" x 50"	5½" x 69"	5½" x 69"	5½" x 84"	7½" x 90"	7½" x 105"
Cut 4 each: Corners	2" x 6"	2 ½" x 7"	2½" x 7"	3½" x 8"	3½" x 8"	3½" x 8"	4½" x 10"	4½" x 10"

Sew the corners to the short sides of the top and bottom inner borders. Press toward the inner borders. Sew the finished top and bottom inner borders to the top and bottom outer borders and press toward the outer borders.

Refer to "Machine Quilting and Attaching the Borders" on page 88.

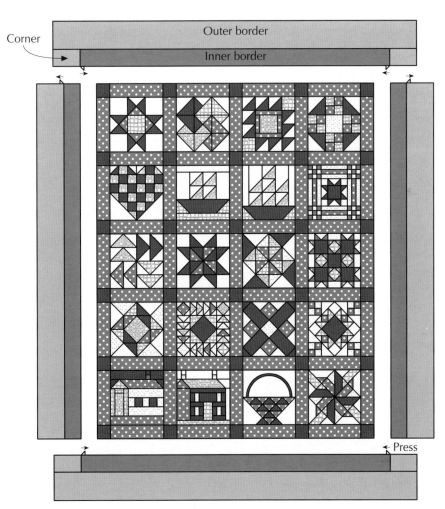

Assembly for Double Border Quilts

Customizing Your Quilt Borders

To customize your borders, start with the borders that correspond with your quilt size. Refer to the charts on page 86. Determine how many inches you want to add or subtract from each border. Call this number X.

Use the following equation to calculate the measurements for a single border.

1. For the sides, the desired width equals X plus or minus the given width. The length does not change.
2. For the top and bottom borders, the desired width equals X plus or minus the given width. The desired length equals 2 times X plus or minus the given length.

For a double border quilt, use the above formula to calculate the measurements for the inner border, then determine how many inches you want to add to or subtract from the outer border. Call this number Y.

1. For the sides, the desired width equals Y plus or minus the given width. The length does not change.
2. For the top and bottom borders, the desired width equals Y plus or minus the given width. If you are increasing the size of your borders, the desired length equals 2 times X plus 2 times Y plus the given length. If you are reducing the size of your borders, the desired length equals 2 times X minus 2 times Y minus the given length.
3. For the corners, the desired width equals the width of your inner border. The length equals the desired width of your outer border plus or minus 2".

For both single and double customized border quilts, cut the backing and the batting pieces 2" wider and longer than your borders.

Machine Quilting and Attaching the Borders

I like to use a simple quilting motif so I only have to start and stop at the ends of the borders. (A template is provided on page 95). Use a copy machine to enlarge the template to fit your quilt. Remember to allow for seam allowances; the template should be about 2½" narrower than the width of your border.

Always quilt the side borders first, then the top and bottom borders.

1. To transfer your quilt pattern, trace it onto tracing paper with a black marker. Put the pattern on a light table or sunny window, place your border fabric on top of the tracing paper, and mark the design with your chalk pencil.
2. On one of the side borders, mark the center of the length. Start marking the border from the center and work toward the ends. Stop marking when you are 2" from each end of the border. Also leave at least 2" free of markings from the edge that will be attached to the sashing and corners.

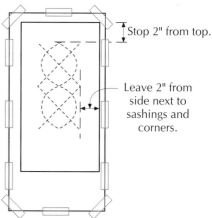

Stop 2" from top.

Leave 2" from side next to sashings and corners.

3. Layer the border on top of the backing and batting and pin well. Machine quilt the cable, always going in the same direction. Don't go down one line, pivot, and then come back; it causes shifting and tucks.
4. Measure the length of your quilt top through the center. Trim the border to the same length as your quilt top. Trim equally from each end.
5. Trim the batting and the backing so that they extend ½" beyond the edges of the long sides of the border.
6. Sew the top layer of the border through all layers of the quilt. Pin the batting and the backing of the border out of the way.
7. Turn the quilt over and lay it flat. Trim the batting even with the raw edge of the stitching that joins the border.
8. Refer to steps 5–6 on page 85. Turn under the backing so that it just covers the stitching (about ⅝"). Pin and machine or hand stitch.
9. Repeat steps 1–8 for the remaining borders.

Binding

I like to use single thickness, straight-grain binding. It is easy to make and economical.

Binding Yardage Chart					
Materials: 44"-wide fabric • *Fabric Requirements in Yards*					
Runner/Wall	**Crib**	**Lap**	**Twin**	**Full/Queen**	**King**
¼	⅜	½	½	½	½

To cut straight-grain binding strips:

1. Measure the sides of your quilt. Add all four measurements plus 10" for seams and corners. This is the amount of binding you need.
2. Cut 1½"-wide strips on the crosswise grain of fabric. (Each strip will be at least 40" long. Divide the length from step 1 by 40" to determine the number of strips you need.)
3. Cut off any selvage edges and sew all the strips together, end to end. Press seams open.
4. Turn one side under 5⁄16" (halfway between ¼" and ⅜") and press for the entire length of the binding.

To attach the binding to your quilt:

1. Trim the quilt batting and backing even with your quilt top.
2. Start near the center of one side of your quilt. Lay the binding, right sides together, on the quilt. Keep the raw edge even with the quilt-top edge. Finger-press the beginning of your binding about ¼". This will finish off your binding edge when you are done.
3. Using a 5⁄16" seam allowance, machine stitch your binding to the quilt. (You may need to adjust the seam allowance to accommodate different thicknesses of batting.) End the stitching 5⁄16" from the corner of the quilt and backstitch.

4. Take the quilt out of the machine. Fold the binding up, away from the quilt.

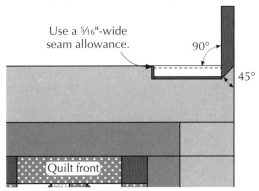

Use a 5⁄16"-wide seam allowance.   90°   45°   Quilt front

5. Fold the binding back onto itself, parallel with the edge of the quilt top. Begin stitching at the edge. End the stitching 5⁄16" from the corner of the quilt and backstitch.

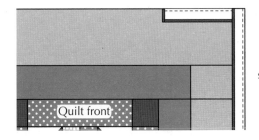

Quilt front

Use a 5⁄16"-wide seam allowance.

6. Repeat steps 4 and 5 for the remaining edges and corners of the quilt. When you reach the beginning of the binding, overlap it about ½" and backstitch. Cut away any excess binding.

7. Fold the binding over the raw edges of the quilt to the back and blindstitch in place. Fold the corners on the back as you go. You may stitch in-the-ditch from the front of the quilt as described on pages 80–81 if you prefer to sew by machine.

Tip

You can make any quilt using this Block by Block method. Just divide the quilt top into small, manageable units and follow the process in this book. I prefer to work with a width of 20" (or less). The length can be the length of the quilt top without borders.

Quilt back

Quilt back

Congratulations, your quilt is done! Add a label, then make a cup of tea or coffee, lay out your quilt, and admire your work.

Meet the Author

Beth shares her Lansing, Michigan, home with her husband, Tom, her daughters, Katy and Colleen, a dog, and a cat. She grew up in a Detroit suburb where she began sewing and quilting while in high school.

A true quilt lover, Beth enjoys all styles of quilts and quilting and tries to learn every new technique available. In addition to quilting, designing, and teaching, she organizes the biannual Northern Michigan Quilters' Getaway in historic Bay View, Michigan.

In developing her designs and Block by Block method for machine quilting, Beth combined her interest in mathematics and drafting with her need to never make the same thing twice!

Photo: Raymond D. Kopen

Block Credits

Album, Beth Donaldson, 1990.

Bow Ties, *Encyclopedia of Pieced Quilt Patterns,* Barbara Brackman, 1993.

Card Trick, *The Perfect Patchwork Primer,* Beth Gutcheon, 1973.

Checkered Heart, Beth Donaldson, 1990.

Devil's Claw, *Encyclopedia of Pieced Quilt Patterns,* Barbara Brackman, 1993.

Diamond Star, *Encyclopedia of Pieced Quilt Patterns,* Barbara Brackman, 1993.

Dutchman's Puzzle, *Encyclopedia of Pieced Quilt Patterns,* Barbara Brackman, 1993.

Goose on the Loose, Beth Donaldson, 1993.

Hanging Basket, *Encyclopedia of Pieced Quilt Patterns,* Barbara Brackman, 1993.

Mother's Fancy Star, *Encyclopedia of Pieced Quilt Patterns,* Barbara Brackman, 1993.

Our Galaxy, Beth Donaldson, 1993.

Peace and Plenty, *Encyclopedia of Pieced Quilt Patterns,* Barbara Brackman, 1993.

Prairie Queen, *Encyclopedia of Pieced Quilt Patterns,* Barbara Brackman, 1993.

Rocking Horse, Beth Donaldson, 1994.

Rocky Mountain Puzzle, *Encyclopedia of Pieced Quilt Patterns,* Barbara Brackman, 1993.

Sailboat, *Encyclopedia of Pieced Quilt Patterns,* Barbara Brackman, 1993.

Sailor's Star, Beth Donaldson, 1994.

Saltbox House, *Patchwork Pictures, 1001 Patterns for Piecing,* Carol LaBranche, 1990.

Schoolhouse, Beth Donaldson, 1990.

Snail's Trail, *Encyclopedia of Pieced Quilt Patterns,* Barbara Brackman, 1993.

Summer's Dream, *Encyclopedia of Pieced Quilt Patterns,* Barbara Brackman, 1993.

Tall Ship, *Encyclopedia of Pieced Quilt Patterns,* Barbara Brackman, 1993.

Variable Star, *The Quilter's Album of Blocks and Borders,* Jinny Beyer.

Whirling Star, *Encyclopedia of Pieced Quilt Patterns,* Barbara Brackman, 1993.

Windblown Square, *Encyclopedia of Pieced Quilt Patterns,* Barbara Brackman, 1993.

Bibliography

Beyer, Jinny. *The Quilter's Album of Blocks and Borders.* McLean, Va.: EPM Publications, Inc., 1986.

Brackman, Barbara. *Encyclopedia of Pieced Quilt Patterns.* Paducah, Ky.: American Quilter's Society, 1993; originally published by Prairie Flower Publishing, 1984.

Gutcheon, Beth. *The Perfect Patchwork Primer.* New York: Penguin Books, 1973.

Hargrave, Harriet. *Heirloom Machine Quilting,* Lafayette, Ca.: C&T Publishing, 1990.

LaBranche, Carol. *Patchwork Pictures, 1001 Patterns for Piecing.* New York: Sterling Publishing, Co., 1990.

Chart Index

Block Index

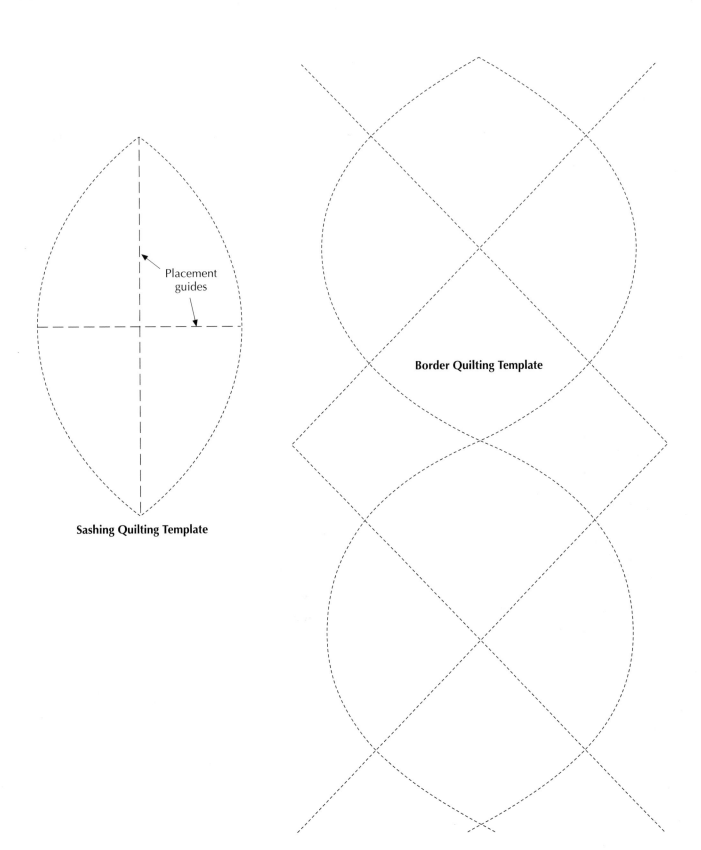

Placement guides

Sashing Quilting Template

Border Quilting Template

That Patchwork Place Publications and Products

All the Blocks Are Geese by Mary Sue Suit
Angle Antics by Mary Hickey
Animas Quilts by Jackie Robinson
Appliqué Borders: An Added Grace
    by Jeana Kimball
Appliqué in Bloom by Gabrielle Swain
Appliquilt™ for Christmas by Tonee White
Appliquilt™: Whimsical One-Step Appliqué
    by Tonee White
Around the Block with Judy Hopkins
Baltimore Bouquets by Mimi Dietrich
Bargello Quilts by Marge Edie
Basic Beauties by Eileen Westfall
Basket Garden by Mary Hickey
Bias Square® Miniatures
    by Christine Carlson
Biblical Blocks by Rosemary Makhan
Block by Block by Beth Donaldson
Borders by Design by Paulette Peters
Botanical Wreaths by Laura M. Reinstatler
Calendar Quilts by Joan Hanson
The Calico House by Joanna Brazier
Cathedral Window: A Fresh Look
    by Nancy J. Martin
The Cat's Meow by Janet Kime
A Child's Garden of Quilts
    by Christal Carter
Colourwash Quilts by Deirdre Amsden
Corners in the Cabin by Paulette Peters
Country Medallion Sampler by Carol Doak
Country Threads by Connie Tesene and
    Mary Tendall
Decoupage Quilts by Barbara Roberts
Designing Quilts by Suzanne Hammond
The Easy Art of Appliqué
    by Mimi Dietrich & Roxi Eppler
Easy Machine Paper Piecing by Carol Doak
Easy Paper-Pieced Keepsake Quilts by
    Carol Doak
Easy Quilts...By Jupiter!®
    by Mary Beth Maison
Easy Reversible Vests by Carol Doak
Fantasy Flowers
    by Doreen Cronkite Burbank
Five- and Seven-Patch Blocks & Quilts
    for the ScrapSaver by Judy Hopkins
Four-Patch Blocks & Quilts for the
    ScrapSaver by Judy Hopkins
Freedom in Design by Mia Rozmyn
Fun with Fat Quarters by Nancy J. Martin
Go Wild with Quilts by Margaret Rolfe
Handmade Quilts by Mimi Dietrich
Happy Endings by Mimi Dietrich
The Heirloom Quilt by Yolande Filson
    and Roberta Przybylski
Holiday Happenings by Christal Carter

In The Beginning by Sharon Evans Yenter
Irma's Sampler by Irma Eskes
Jacket Jazz by Judy Murrah
Jacket Jazz Encore by Judy Murrah
The Joy of Quilting by Joan Hanson &
    Mary Hickey
Le Rouvray by Diane de Obaldia,
    with Marie-Christine Flocard
    and Cosabeth Parriaud
Lessons in Machine Piecing
    by Marsha McCloskey
Little Quilts by Alice Berg, Sylvia Johnson,
    and Mary Ellen Von Holt
Lively Little Logs by Donna McConnell
Loving Stitches by Jeana Kimball
Machine Quilting Made Easy
    by Maurine Noble
Make Room for Quilts by Nancy J. Martin
Nifty Ninepatches by Carolann M. Palmer
Nine-Patch Blocks & Quilts for the
    ScrapSaver by Judy Hopkins
Not Just Quilts by Jo Parrott
Oh! Christmas Trees
    compiled by Barbara Weiland
On to Square Two by Marsha McCloskey
Osage County Quilt Factory
    by Virginia Robertson
Our Pieceful Village by Lynn Rice
Painless Borders by Sally Schneider
Patchwork Basics by Marie-Christine
    Flocard & Cosabeth Parriaud
A Perfect Match by Donna Lynn Thomas
Picture Perfect Patchwork
    by Naomi Norman
Piecemakers® Country Store
    by the Piecemakers
Pineapple Passion
    by Nancy Smith and Lynda Milligan
A Pioneer Doll and Her Quilts
    by Mary Hickey
Pioneer Storybook Quilts by Mary Hickey
Prairie People—Cloth Dolls to Make
    and Cherish by Marji Hadley and
    J. Dianne Ridgley
Quick & Easy Quiltmaking by Mary Hickey,
    Nancy J. Martin, Marsha McCloskey
    and Sara Nephew
The Quilt Room by Pam Lintott and
    Rosemary Miller
The Quilted Apple by Laurene Sinema
Quilted for Christmas
    compiled by Ursula Reikes
Quilted for Christmas, Book II
    compiled by Christine Barnes and
    Barbara Weiland
Quilted Sea Tapestries by Ginny Eckley

The Quilters' Companion
    compiled by That Patchwork Place
The Quilting Bee
    by Jackie Wolff and Lori Aluna
Quilting Makes the Quilt by Lee Cleland
Quilts for All Seasons by Christal Carter
Quilts for Baby: Easy as A, B, C
    by Ursula Reikes
Quilts for Kids by Carolann M. Palmer
Quilts from Nature by Joan Colvin
Quilts to Share by Janet Kime
Red Wagon Originals
    by Gerry Kimmel and Linda Brannock
Rotary Riot
    by Judy Hopkins and Nancy J. Martin
Rotary Roundup
    by Judy Hopkins and Nancy J. Martin
Round About Quilts by J. Michelle Watts
Round Robin Quilts
    by Pat Magaret and Donna Slusser
Samplings from the Sea
    by Rosemary Makhan
ScrapMania by Sally Schneider
Seasoned with Quilts by Retta Warehime
Sensational Settings by Joan Hanson
Sewing on the Line
    by Lesly-Claire Greenberg
Shortcuts: A Concise Guide to Rotary
    Cutting by Donna Lynn Thomas
Shortcuts Sampler by Roxanne Carter
Shortcuts to the Top
    by Donna Lynn Thomas
Small Talk by Donna Lynn Thomas
Smoothstitch® Quilts by Roxi Eppler
The Stitchin' Post
    by Jean Wells and Lawry Thorn
Stringing Along by Trice Boerens
Sunbonnet Sue All Through the Year
    by Sue Linker
Tea Party Time by Nancy J. Martin
Template-Free® Quiltmaking
    by Trudie Hughes
Template-Free® Quilts and Borders
    by Trudie Hughes
Template-Free® Stars by Jo Parrott
Through the Window & Beyond
    by Lynne Edwards
Treasures from Yesteryear, Book One
    by Sharon Newman
Treasures from Yesteryear, Book Two
    by Sharon Newman
Two for Your Money by Jo Parrott
Watercolor Quilts
    by Pat Magaret and Donna Slusser
Woven & Quilted by Mary Anne Caplinger

4", 6", 8", & metric Bias Square® • BiRangle™ • Ruby Beholder™ • Pineapple Rule • ScrapMaster • Rotary Rule™ • Rotary Mate™
Shortcuts to America's Best-Loved Quilts (video)

Many titles are available at your local quilt shop. For more information, send $2 for a color catalog to
That Patchwork Place, Inc., PO Box 118, Bothell WA 98041-0118 USA.

☎ Call 1-800-426-3126 for the name and location of the quilt shop nearest you.